D0464597

DATE DUE			JUN 0 5
JUL 0 9 '05			
7/19			
NOV 0 2 '05			
JUN 2 7 2006			
OCT 1 8 '08			
GAYLORD			PRINTED IN U.S.A.

In Search of Sacred Places
Looking for Wisdom on Celtic Holy Islands

IN SEARCH OF SACRED PLACES

Looking for Wisdom on Celtic Holy Islands

DANIEL TAYLOR

 BOG WALK PRESS

JACKSON COUNTY LIBRARY SERVICES
MEDFORD OREGON 97501

Copyright © 2005 Daniel Taylor

All rights reserved. No part of this book may be used or reproduced in any manner whatsoever without the written permission of the Publisher.

Published by Bog Walk Press
1605 Lake Johanna Blvd.
Saint Paul, MN 55112
651.638.6357

Cover and book design by Matthew Taylor,
Taylor Design Works, LLC

Excerpt from "Llananno" in *Collected Poems 1945-1990*
by R. S. Thomas, Phoenix, London, 1995.
© Kunjana Thomas 2001, used by permission.

Bible translations by the author.

ISBN: 0-9706511-1-2

*For all spiritual questers who suspect there might be
more to things than what we see.
And for Arthur Lynip, an early model and borderline saint.*

ACKNOWLEDGMENTS

Many hands and heads contributed to the incarnation of this book. I would like to thank the Bethel University Alumni Committee for a grant to go, John Wilson for telling me to write it down, Gérard Pierre for encouraging words, Mary Ellen Ashcroft for a perceptive critique, David Healy for skillful editing, Matthew Taylor for an excellent design, Barbara Leafblad, Daniel Perego, and Des Lavelle for their evocative photographs, and Rick Halverson, Alberto Bonacina, and Giorgio Fumagalli for technical help. Thanks also to the "Celtic group"–Freemans, Leafblads and McCloskeys–for patient and perceptive listening.

CONTENTS

Whan that Aprille, with his shoures sote,
The droghte of March hath perced to the rote ...
Thanne longen folk to goon on pilgrimages.
    The Canterbury Tales

Stand at the crossroads and look around.
Ask for the old paths that lead to good.
Walk them and you will find rest for your souls.
    Jeremiah 6:16

Skellig Michael is a 700-foot-high pinnacle of water-and-wind-worn rock that rises like Excalibur out of the Atlantic waves off the southwest coast of Ireland. If you have ever been there, you do not need it described; if you have not been, no description is adequate. The same is true of that part of reality called the sacred—a quality of being that is sometimes wedded to physical places, places like Skellig Michael. If you have been in the vicinity of the sacred—ever brushed against the holy—you retain it more in your bones than in your head; and if you haven't, no description of the experience will ever be satisfactory.

But I didn't start my travels with the idea of visiting Skellig Michael, or with any intention of getting tangled up with holy places. I was simply going to England in the springtime to spend a few weeks studying Sir Thomas More, a personal hero. Armed with a $1,000 grant from the Alumni Committee, I was going to look around London, take a few notes, snap a few pictures, come back and turn it all into all into serviceable prose for a serviceable book, marking the passing of another year in my serviceable life.

A few months before going, however, I got diverted by the Celtic saints. A colleague in California told me I must go to Iona in Scotland, a mystical place he said. "I've taken students there twice," he told me. "Each time when we left they stood on the opposite shore and stared back in silence at the island and did not want to get on the bus to leave."

So I tucked away the idea of visiting Iona if I could, and thought I may as well see Lindisfarne in northern England at the same time. From a book I bought while on Iona, I found out about St. David's in Wales and Glendalough, south of Dublin. And there was also a brief reference to an isolated spike of towering rock in the seas off the Ring of Kerry called Skellig Michael. I didn't plan on going to any of them. I thought I would perhaps take a quick look at Iona and Lindisfarne, but then stick with Sir Thomas More. But in going to Iona–as a detached observer–I was, unawares, beginning a pilgrimage.

Or was I?

Most writing on pilgrimage makes a distinction between the pilgrim and the tourist. The tourist goes to see and collect (memories and mementos); the pilgrim goes to be changed. I was, by this definition, clearly a tourist. Unlike my wife, who sees each day as an opportunity to improve herself and those around her, I contemplate personal change with no enthusiasm. It's taken me half a century to reach my present state, such as it is, and wanting to be different strikes me as a form of ingratitude. Be careful what you wish for, I think; try to change me and I could easily get worse.

But then I come across a definition of pilgrim as one who travels hopefully. That seems right, within my reach–and sufficiently vague. I could go to Iona with a certain anticipation that attends forays into the unfamiliar. Such anticipation suggests not merely curiosity, but an inclination toward finding something good and helpful in the unknown.

If pilgrims travel hopefully, what are they hoping for? To meet God, many say. This raises a central irony of pilgrimage. Most religions, certainly mine, teach that God is available everywhere. Why, then, should I go to Iona to find God rather than to my bedroom closet? Thoreau asked 150 years ago why westerners get so excited about exploring the blank places on the maps of Africa when there are such large stretches of white space on our inner maps. And when everyone else was gung-ho for pilgrimage in the Middle Ages, the Cistercian monks did not permit them, calling instead for an inner journey in imitation of Christ. God is not any more, or less, on Iona than in my garage. And yet no one has reported an intense religious experience in my garage, and many have done so after visiting Iona.

Perhaps this is why we go in search of sacred places. If we are looking for gold, we listen when someone tells us where they've found gold. If we are looking for God, we listen when someone reports to have felt God close in a certain place. Such news is precious. We have always sought it out, and we always will.

There is, then, something both individual and communal about seeking the holy through pilgrimage. Each pilgrim goes individually to find God, to find meaning, or, at least, to fulfill some indefinite hope. And yet we often go together, with other pilgrims, or, even if alone, where others have gone before us. Like travelers in a dense forest, we are thankful for a worn path, for marks carved on a tree, for any hint that we are moving in the right direction.

chapter one

To Iona – An Island Off an Island Off an Island

The Lord said to Abram, "Leave your country and your kindred and your father's house and go to the land I will show you."

Genesis 12:1

Let us leave Derry of the Oaks,
With sadness, tears and a heavy heart;
Our hearts break to depart so,
To go away to live with strangers.

Attributed to Columba on leaving Ireland

The journey to a sacred place is as important as the place itself. Traveling is an action – of the body and of the will – in the direction of a desired destination. The act of going is itself a vote for the possibility of meaning. It accepts risk – the risk of coming to harm, of being a fool, of wasting time and money and energy – for the mere possibility of a highly intangible reward.

In my case, it also entails travel in a very overloaded van. Seven of us – wife, four children, and new daughter-in-law–head out in late March from the southern coast of England in a vehicle that, like the holy, has to be experienced to be understood. It is a used Toyota van with more miles on it than the odometer cares to admit. It is multicolored, the result of replaced panels from past encounters, but gives the general impression of being dull gold. The fellow at the used car rental agency tries to explain its idiosyncrasies to me. "Push just here when you slide the door close or it won't catch." "The interior lights use up the battery, so we've disconnected them." Then he mutters something about the poorly designed cooling system on this model.

But one thing I like about the van is its name–Space Cruiser. Apparently a lot of cars in Britain include the term space in their name. A friend there has a car called a Space Wagon. But it strikes my American ear as funny, and I can't help thinking of Star Wars. I am going to pilgrimage to Scotland in my battered Space Cruiser just as an interplanetary cargo ship might ferry its load to distant Tatooine.

We pile luggage for seven in the back and on top of the van. I've purchased a blue tarp and bungee cords at a junk place near the Lymington harbor called Yacht Grot. Fully loaded, the van's nose is pointed, appropriately, toward the sky. I get in the driver's seat, start the engine, and call out, "Space Cruiser–to Iona and beyond!" Chaucer's motley crew of pilgrims has nothing on us.

✝ ✝ ✝

Pilgrimage is physical travel with a spiritual destination. The first recorded postbiblical Christian pilgrimage took place around A.D. 170 when Melito of Sardis went to Jerusalem to see if he could confirm the gospel stories. But the Bible itself is filled with pilgrimages. Abraham left Ur at God's behest, looking for a city "whose builder and maker is God." The Israelites embarked on a forty-year pilgrimage whose goal was the Promised Land. Paul's missionary journeys were a special kind of pilgrimage. And Jesus himself was killed on a pilgrimage—the annual Passover pilgrimage to Jerusalem.

What happened to Jesus reveals something about pilgrimages that not many people understand anymore: Pilgrimages can be dangerous. Many medieval pilgrims wrote out wills before going, often leaving their possessions to the local church, and a great number of them never made it back. Some people found them so frightening—or inconvenient—that they hired professional pilgrims to go to holy places for them to earn vicarious credit (much as today we too often go to church to watch others perform worship for us).

The dangers now are primarily spiritual. The greatest danger of pilgrimage, always, is the temptation to live off someone else's experience with transcendence. We go to Iona because St. Columba was there and reportedly talked to the angels. We go to Lindisfarne because St. Cuthbert healed the sick. We go to Skellig Michael because anyone who would choose to live there during an Irish winter must be very close to God—or very disturbed.

At our most insecure, we want to materialize and quantify the holy so we can keep an eye on it. Quantification provides a kind of control. And so we make a game of this quest for transcendence. In the Middle Ages, pilgrimages earned you points with God. Trips to Jerusalem or Rome were spiritual touchdowns, worth the most points. You could score field goals and safeties too. Three trips to Glendalough in Ireland were said to be worth one to Rome. But you could earn the equivalent with only two trips to St. David's in Wales.

I find myself veering toward sarcasm. This is the Texas Baptist residue left in my bones. I was raised by one of the few groups in Christendom who eschew sacred traveling. For us reared in Protestant fundamentalism, the word saint could only be followed by the word Paul—or a small handful of other biblical names. Anything else put us in mind of the Antichrist. Even now, many years removed in time and outlook from my upbringing, I find it strange to be standing in Kildare asking locals where to find St. Brigid's well. The very idea of holy wells would have given my Sunday School teachers heartburn, and there are reported to be 3,000 such wells in Ireland alone.

We Texas Baptists didn't go on pilgrimages, but we did, in our own way, believe in the notion of pilgrimage. Didn't we sing, "This world is not my home, I'm just a passin' through"? Didn't the Bible say that all people of faith are "strangers and pilgrims on the earth"? Perhaps we didn't go on earthly pilgrimages because we knew this whole life is nothing but one long pilgrimage toward God. Or perhaps it was because we had our suspicions about holiness, and weren't too keen on finding it.

✝ ✝ ✝

Iona is a long way from our start in southern England—in many ways. One day of driving gets us to the Lake District and a second well into the Scottish Highlands. Something in the feel of things changes north of Glasgow. The Highland mountains are small by world standards, but they are abrupt and desolate and crowd around you on the narrow road. And in the early spring, when winter has not completely let them go, they can be forbidding. They seem to ask why you—you in the van with the flapping blue tarp—why have you come here out of season, and what do you expect to find?

At the end of two days driving we are in Oban, a small town on the sea. We are still two ferry rides and a number of mind sets away from Iona. The following morning we put the Space Cruiser on a car ferry to the island of Mull. The road across Mull to the south and west is a single lane, with regular turnouts to allow for oncoming vehicles. Each turnout is marked by a tall pole, undoubtedly helpful for staying on track when there is snow.

Mull is like the Highlands in miniature—empty seeming, almost lunar in its desolate beauty, yet full of stubborn life for those with eyes to see. We drive for an hour to reach the other side of the island. There is no warning of what is approaching until we drive into the village of Fionnphort. There, suddenly, surprisingly close across a narrow stretch of water, is Iona and the Abbey, the latter built on the site where Columba worshiped so many centuries ago. Having been thinking about finding gas and making the next ferry, I am not prepared to reach the goal of my pilgrimage. Here is the long-sought sacred place and I am not ready.

✜ ✜ ✜

Looking at Iona across the half mile of water that separates it from Mull, I have the feeling I am looking at a movie set or one of those miniature model towns of which the English are so fond. I can see almost the length of the island—three and a half miles from end to end. The restored Abbey toward the north end dominates the view, as it does most pilgrims' perceptions of Iona. Directly across the water are the few houses and small buildings that make up the village.

And behind it all rises the hill of Dun I *(done ee)*, the highest point at 330 feet of a hump of rock and grass that dominates the northern half of the island. The entire island is colored in shades of light greens and grays, neither lush nor barren, speaking of possibilities for life that are genuine but rigorous.

Because visitors are not allowed to bring cars onto Iona, we park the Space Cruiser and walk down to the small ferry. As we pass over the sound to the island, I reflect on the stages of travel that have brought me to Iona: to England by jet, to Cambridge by train, to the south coast and then Oban by car, to Mull by car ferry, and now on to Iona by passenger ferry. And then, while on Iona, only by foot. This physical progression is the outward dimension of a necessary process of shedding that must go on at many levels if one is to approach the sacred. My technological crutches become ever more simple and then disappear—plane, train, car, ferry, feet. The physical scale continually shrinks—from North American continent to island nation to small island of Mull to tiny island of Iona.

An island off an island off an island—it feels as if I am approaching the edge of something. And I am not altogether happy about it. I am sure it is not only external things—planes and Space Cruisers—that must be shed. Surely an inward kind of giving up and simplifying is also required if I am to be more than a tourist, or fact-finder, on Iona. And that of course would be uncomfortable.

✛ ✛ ✛

We have come to Iona only because someone else did—more than 1,400 years ago. I cannot comprehend that many years on a human scale, but I can comprehend his human motivation, human nature having changed not at all since Adam. He came to get away from something, hoping to find something else.

In Ireland he is known as Colum-cille—Dove of the Church—and as Columba to most of the rest of the world. As was the case for many who became monks during the flowering of Celtic Christianity, he came from the best of families, in fact from Irish nobility. Columba was born in A.D. 521 in northwestern Ireland into the powerful Ui Neill clan, a clan whose leaders often contested with other clans to be one of the high kings of Ireland.

Columba began training for the church as a boy, a not uncommon practice in a world where childhood was very short and roles in life were usually decided at birth. Not much is known of the first part of his adult life, though he is credited with founding monasteries at Derry in 546 and Durrow in 556.

Columba did not embark on the adventure that made him famous until past the age of forty, a comforting thought for those of us in the second half of life who wonder if we have left any footprints. In 563 he left Ireland for Scotland, "wishing to be a pilgrim for Christ." So wrote Adomnan, his seventh-century biographer. Some people attribute to him less flattering motivations. And at least one of them lives on Iona today.

✠ ✠ ✠

When we walk onto Iona from the ferry, we are greeted by Mrs. MacCormick, a sheep-farming woman from whom we have rented a cottage. She welcomes us in a soft swell of a voice whose rhythmic lilt is thousands of years old, though it has accommodated itself to English on the island only in the last century. Taking my wife Jayne and the luggage in her car, she directs the rest of us to walk south on the only road on the island. "Go here past Martyrs' Bay and keep walking until you see my car outside the cottage." She doesn't warn us about the troll.

The six of us walk past the war memorial at Martyrs' Bay—so called because sixty-eight monks are said to have been slaughtered there by Viking raiders in 806—and then past Little Rock, Port of Hummocks, and Row You Can't Row Skerry. All are translations of originally Gaelic names like Iomair Cha'n Iomair Sgeir that both beckon the ear and scare the tongue away. The Celtic love of words survives today even in Iona guidebooks, one of which describes a local attraction as follows: "The Spouting Cave performs most dramatically at about half-tide when there is a shapely sea fetching from the west," a sentence itself both shapely and fetching.

The road, after a few hundred yards of running parallel to the sound, turns right and we follow it up what the map refers to as Ascent of the Tillage Plot. Here we meet the troll. He has laid out bait for us at the opening to his lair in the form of crudely carved pieces of stone sitting in a box by his fence at the edge of the road. More carvings, with a variety of Celtic designs and crosses, lie by the path leading from his fence to his door, where still more can be found on the porch. There hasn't been such a clearly marked path to destruction since Hansel and Gretel's bread crumbs.

I call him a troll because it gives me pleasure to do so and because it seems fitting for a pilgrimage to a Celtic place. The troll is actually an old man who takes it as his role to be the resident Iona debunker. And therefore I like him. He spots us from inside his house as we look at his carvings at the fence, and invites us to the porch to see more. He knows why we've come to Iona and wastes no time launching into his routine.

"As far as I can see, Columba was a loud-mouthed bigot."

This is not what we flew between two continents, drove two days in the Space Cruiser, and rode two ferries to hear. But there is more.

"There were already priests here when he arrived, and he kicked them out, along with all the women. He only came because he had started a battle over a book back in Ireland. Thousands of men were killed, so he had to come here to get away."

Like much in the popular view of Celtic Christianity, the old man's views combine smatterings of historical fact with large amounts of conjecture, legend, and personal prejudices. He is right about a strong tradition linking Columba to books. Before leaving Ireland, Columba is said to have borrowed (or stolen) a book of the Psalms from St. Finnian and copied it without his permission. Finnian was outraged when he found out and demanded the copy as well as the original. Columba refused to return the copy on the grounds that he intended to use it for good and that the original was unharmed. So the matter went to court.

The judge's decision is famous: "To every cow its calf, and to every book its copy." The copy was deemed to belong to Finnian. Columba reputedly still refused to return it, and a battle ensued in which Columba helped his clan achieve victory, perhaps by standing behind the fighting warriors with arms upraised, beseeching heaven. So goes one version of the story.

Although the troll does not guess it, I love Columba more, not less, for his passion for a book. Oh that we went today to court or battle over love of books! What was the nature of his failing? Was it a sin of love? Of desire? Of mere acquisitiveness—a fine book being then a rare and beautiful treasure? Perhaps all three, mixed together with the hope of better worshiping God.

The battle took place under the shadow of Ben Bulben, a small mountain near Sligo in western Ireland where fights took place in the uncountable past among the heroes of Celtic legend. I have sometimes taken students there to see the grave of W. B. Yeats. This battle that some link to

Columba's book copying, however, was no legend. Several thousand men were killed. A medieval tradition ties this event with a church synod not long after and suggests that Columba was ordered out of Ireland. Score one for the troll.

It is also true that Iona was not empty when Columba arrived. The Celts had come to Scotland by 4500 B.C. and had been farming on Iona from perhaps 2500 B.C. There is inconclusive evidence that Iona may have even been a holy place long before Christianity existed. Standing stones are common on Mull and some have claimed that a series of them marks a route from the eastern edge of the island to the very place where one disembarks for Iona today. We may be in a longer line of pilgrims coming to Iona than anyone knows.

There even were Christians on Iona before Columba's arrival, and some may not have been all that happy to see him (that part of Scotland had been settled from Ireland earlier by a rival clan to Columba's). Further, many of the scores of superficial treatments of the Celtic saints repeat the story that Columba kicked all the women off the island by banning cows, saying, "Where there is a cow, there is a woman, and where there is a woman, there is mischief." Score two more for the troll.

So go the legends, but in fact there is no historical proof for any of them, nor any convincing evidence of a link among the battle, the synod, and Columba's departure. The saying about cows and women is a traditional one that got attached to Columba long after his death, and no other stories about his life support a distrust or hatred of women.

In fact, one story from Adomnan describes Columba suddenly standing up one day and announcing, "Now I must hurry to the church to beseech God on behalf of a poor girl who is tortured by the pains of a most difficult childbirth and who now in Ireland calls on my name." He "was moved to pity for the girl and ran to the church," where he prayed for her until he sensed that she had given birth and was out of danger.

What seems most likely is that Columba was an intelligent, forceful man of high birth who turned away from the life of a warrior noble that could conceivably have led to his becoming a high king of Ireland. In its place he sought a life of devotion to God and to service. He was apparently a physically strong man with a voice loud enough to call to people on the opposite shore across the Iona sound. He loved books and learning and poetry and songs. He may well have carried with him a temper that led to actions he regretted. Perhaps he did feel some responsibility for others losing their lives, or at least for not doing enough to stop it. Or maybe, as some have speculated, he simply wanted to get away from it all—from family, from politics, from synods, from human machinations of all kinds—and see if he couldn't live a little closer to God.

All of which is to say that Columba was quite human. Maybe the Iona debunker was right. Maybe Columba was a loudmouth bigot. Or perhaps the old man was actually describing himself. But if Columba was undoubtedly flawed, that makes him more useful as a saint and an object of pilgrimage than otherwise.

I like my saints to be scoundrels, or at least have the

potential for it, because I know I am a scoundrel myself. The hope provided by the lives of saints comes not because they are unfallen but because being fallen does not prevent them from living faithful and powerful lives. A saint who never lost his temper or never had to overcome the desire to sleep through morning prayers can offer me little encouragement for my own imperfect life.

So I silently thank the old man for his intolerance. It shakes a little of the romantic veneer off my pilgrimage, reminding me that one man's saint is another man's rogue. The things I seek in this world are not sought by everyone, not even on the holy island of Iona.

✚ ✚ ✚

We have arrived at lambing time. The first lamb of the season for the MacCormick's was born during the night, so Mr. MacCormick has had no sleep. I get directions to the only grocery store on the island and go to get bread and milk and something to cook for dinner. When I get there, however, the Spar store is closed. It doesn't look good for dinner, or breakfast either for that matter. I look in the locked door and see a young woman sweeping up. Back home it would be no use trying to get her attention. She would only point to the sign posting the store hours and shake her head. The cash register would already be locked and she would have places she needed to get to. But this is Iona and so I knock. The young woman comes and opens the door and I ask if I can still buy some food. She invites me in and continues sweeping while I shop.

This is no small thing. Which is to say, it is a small

thing but not a trivial thing. She has reflexively met another person's minor need, without thought for rules or her own convenience. In so doing she keeps alive into another century the oft-noted Celtic tradition of hospitality. Such hospitality predates Christianity but receives a theological underpinning in an ancient Celtic poem:

> *O King of stars!*
> *Whether my home be dark or bright,*
> *Never shall it be closed against anyone,*
> *Lest Christ close His home against me.*

Is it too dreamy to ask why we need homeless shelters when the suburbs are so full of empty bedrooms? Am I ready to begin with my own?

✝ ✝ ✝

Columba brought twelve other monks to Iona with him in one of the sea-going coracles that the Celts used to sail throughout that part of the world (and, according to legend, that St. Brendan the Navigator sailed all the way to America). There may well have been more people in the boat with them, but for later hagiographers the official number was thirteen to echo Christ and his disciples.

Columba wanted to go far enough away that he could not see Ireland from his new home, and so rejected an earlier landing place further south. After sailing into what became Columba's Bay on the southern end of the island, he climbed up the highest nearby hill and looked back over the sea. Satisfied that Ireland could not be seen, he declared this island the place they would start their monastic life together. That hill has long been called Cairn of the Back to Ireland, otherwise translated as Look Back to Ireland, or, in contrast, Back Turned to Ireland.

However one translates it, the significance is the same. There is a no-looking-back quality to the wanderings of the Celtic Christians that is both admirable and frightening. Of the three kinds of martyrdom the Celts identified – red, green, and white – the white martyrdom was considered the most difficult. The red martyrdom was death by the shedding of blood that the Celtic Christians most envied in earlier Christian history but only occasionally experienced themselves. One of the remarkable features of the Christianizing of Ireland and Scotland is that it occurred without violence, a credit both to the pagans who considered the message and to the Christians who brought it.

The green martyrdom was the decision to live with self-imposed deprivation, usually in isolation – Skellig Michael offers a prime example. It was the martyrdom of the hermitage and of extreme, penitential asceticism. The green martyr was the one set apart (the root meaning of holy) even from others who had chosen to be set apart. The hermitage of the green martyr could literally be only yards away from where others lived, but it was perceived as light years away in spiritual space.

The white martyrdom was the decision to trust one's fate to the God of the winds and tides, to be a peregrinatio – a wanderer for God. Often the white martyrs did not know exactly where they were going. Some sailed to a specific place, others in a general direction, and a few didn't bother with sails at all. They simply got in their small boats and allowed the wind and currents to take them. Wherever they landed they brought the good news of the gospel to whomever they found; that place they now called home.

It was a frightening prospect to leave home and trust oneself to the winds, as can be seen in words attributed to St. Brendan: "Shall I abandon, O King of Mysteries, the soft comforts of home? ... Shall I go of my own choice upon the sea? O Christ, will you help me on the wild waves?"

The white martyrdom was thought the most difficult not only because it was dangerous but also because the original Celtic missionaries so loved their native Ireland and kin. They chose this form of martyrdom because they wished to suffer as Christ had suffered. Nothing could be more painful than separation from land and loved ones. The Irish in general took great pleasure in their green land and in its songs and storytelling and arts and hearth. Even monks who were separated from their families tended to identify strongly with a local people. Only the greatest sense of call and duty could pry them away.

So though Iona is less than a hundred miles from Ireland by sea, Columba's leave-taking was painful and assumed to be permanent. Christ warns against taking the hand from the plow once one has chosen the life of faith. Celtic missionaries, who took the gospel to Scotland, then throughout Europe to as far as Russia, usually left thinking they would never return. Columba may even have vowed not to touch Irish soil again. (One doubtful story says that when he did, in fact, make a necessary trip back to Ireland later in life, he tied Iona sod to the bottom of his sandals and had himself blindfolded in an attempt to keep his vow.)

The integrity and courage required for the white martyrdom, implied in the name Cairn of the Back to Ireland, is admirable. It calls to mind biblical stories such as the pearl of great price for which one sacrifices everything, or the passage in Luke 5 that describes the response of Peter, John, and James when Christ calls to them in their fishing boats to be his disciples: "And when they had brought their boats to land, they left everything, and followed him." The same could be said of Columba and the twelve who landed in that pebbly Iona bay.

But if admirable, such single-mindedness is also frightening. We moderns and postmoderns like to keep our options open, to try things out, to see if something feels "right for me." We tend to choose our religion, like our wardrobes and worldviews, cafeteria style, taking a bit of this and a bit of that, skipping over anything that looks unappetizing or hard to digest. We might occasionally take a chance on something unfamiliar, knowing we can throw it away if a small taste doesn't suit us.

The truth is, I find the level of devotion of these saints unsettling. Admirable and inspiring, perhaps, but ultimately unsettling. Their devotion condemns me, as all extremism does. They go too far, they aren't normal, they lack a sense of proportion. I want them to take life a little easier, because that's how I want to take life myself—easy. I agree with the Japanese man who was discomfited when he first heard about Jesus: "I read in a book that a man called Christ went about doing good. It was very disconcerting to me that I am so easily satisfied with just going about."

Saints are fine as distant examples, but I don't want to

live with them. I am more at home with those hibernators under the snow who complain that "April is the cruelest month." Spring may have excited Chaucer's pilgrims to "goon on pilgrimages," but T. S. Eliot knew that we modern folk prefer to be covered "in forgetful snow, feeding/ A little life with dried tubers." Saints are spiritual terrorists, trying to blow us up with their messages from God. How can I relax and putter contentedly along when the person next to me is having visions? It's too extreme. It's not polite.

Maybe that's what my students feel when they wrinkle up their noses on hearing about monastic life. "We shouldn't withdraw from the world," they say. "We should be involved." Sometimes they use the word *reality* instead of *world* and suggest that the monastic types are trying to escape from it. But charging someone with trying to escape from reality requires that you yourself know what is real. Calling someone an extremist suggests you are confident about where the center is, the center by which the extreme is defined. A literary critic has said that for experimental writers and artists, extremism is simply a method for searching for what is real. Saints and spiritual explorers are searching for the same thing.

Does the person who thinks that hours in prayer every day are a retreat from reality believe that hours at an office desk are closer to reality? Or at a mall? If entering into formal worship seven times a day is extreme, is watching television every day something that moves us to the center of life? If we claim that the monastic life isn't practical in our day, we should ask ourselves, "practical for accomplishing what?" What is the goal toward which the practice of life should direct us, by which practical or impractical is measured?

Often when we use terms like real or practical, we actually mean familiar. Whatever is normal, the experience of the majority, we call real; whatever is rare, especially in behavior, is extreme. Whatever conforms to how we presently organize our lives is practical; whatever challenges that organization is not. As Emily Dickinson noted, "Much Madness is divinest Sense – / To a discerning Eye," adding, "'Tis the Majority/ In this, as All, prevail." Living in the light of eternity is, apparently, highly impractical.

And yet I have to admit that I am inclined to vote with the majority when it comes to some aspects of the lives of these extremists. Columba used a stone for a pillow. He prayed for nights at a time without sleep. He fasted like food would poison his soul (and he was a glutton compared to some of the other Celtic saints). Stone pillows, freezing cells, days without food and nights without sleep. Is this life? How does this honor a good and generous God? I'm not sure, in all cases, that it does. It appears that at times they were trying to earn something that can only be given. They wouldn't be human if they didn't occasionally make this mistake.

But I should not let myself too quickly off the hook. If they were sometimes too extreme, why am I never extreme at all? If they hated too bitterly their daily human failings, why do I hate mine so little – preferring instead to excuse and stroke and nurture them?

Their extreme example should, at the least, call me out

of the bubble of comfort and excuse I have created for myself, with the smiling encouragement of a hedonistic culture. As I stand at the place where Columba's cell once stood, I do not feel I must become Columba. I do, however, feel I must learn something from him, something from his pilgrimage in the sixth century for my pilgrimage through life here at the beginning of the twenty-first.

✝ ✝ ✝

After supper we decide to take a hike. We are unaware that we are about to fulfill the traditional expectation that a pilgrimage include suffering, in imitation of the suffering of Christ on the way to the cross. Fortunately it is a very low level of suffering compatible with modern weakness.

From the road just beyond the Cathedral, we first take the relatively easy path up to the top of Dun I. The views from there are spectacular in each direction—Mull and the mountains of the Highlands to the east; the islands of Coll, Tralee, and Staffa to the north; Islay to the south; and to the west Dutchman's Cap and the open sea. A bonfire was built up here to announce the end of World War II, a modern instance of an ancient practice.

The seven of us scurry around the top of Dun I for a bit and then gather for the requisite group photo. We have conquered a three-hundred-foot Scottish mountain and we are proud. I gather everyone by the large rock that tops the hill and sight them through my camera, balancing it on the same rock a few feet away. I push the timer button and dash to join my family, an action that never fails to result in a picture of smilers.

And we have reason to smile. We are with the people we love, we are having adventures, and we are, largely unawares, on a pilgrimage. What could be better?

Well, one thing could have been better. We could have gone down the same way we came up. Instead, my instinct for shortcuts takes over. My map indicates a walking path down the southwest side of the peak, and I put in a vote for variety. Plus it looks like a shorter way back to our cottage. Annie, our youngest, counsels us to return down the east side, the way we came up. Do not neglect the wisdom of twelve-year-olds.

Adventure trumps prudence and we take off. It looks easy on the map–a gentle walk between Hill of the Cock and Hill of the Bends, then across the Meadow of the Lapwings, past the Signal Burial Ground and through Eithne's Fold to home base. The map doesn't indicate the mud, the fences, or the complete lack of signage.

Here at the high point on the island the ground oozes water. The trail we start down ends in just a few yards. That should tell me that many start this way and then, after seeing how unpromising things look, come back. Instead, the end of the trail says to me, "Fare forward, valiant pilgrim. Only the worthy can hope to walk in the footsteps of saints!"

Within a few minutes of losing the trail we are all faring forward in different directions. Matt and wife Sarah are off to my right, Nate and Julie are somewhere to my left, and Jayne and Anne are hanging back altogether to see who disappears into sinkholes first. Anne is warming up for the first "I told you so" of a series.

Apparently the possibility of a muddy, watery death is not enough testing for God. For some reason there are also barbed wire fences up here, at the most inconvenient places. I tear my new jeans climbing over the first one we come to. I begin wondering how it is possible to feel lost on an island this small, and then remember that the earth is only a tiny dot in the universe and yet many people feel lost on it.

A few minutes after tearing my jeans, I lose a tennis shoe to the muck. It is sucked off my foot when I try jumping from one bit of dry ground to another, and the muck will not give it back even when I turn and pull on the shoe with all my strength. Only when I take a stick and jab under the shoe to release the vacuum does Iona grudgingly return its prize.

What looked to be a twenty-minute stroll becomes a ninety-minute survival trek. The sun is going down but our spirits are not. We invoke the family tradition of christening any extended miscalculation as, officially, An Adventure. I dub this The Bog Walk, worthy of any chronicle of middle-earth, and it is now immortalized in our collective memories. We have a story worthy of a pilgrimage.

✠ ✠ ✠

Everything on Iona has a name. Each physical feature of the island has been part of a specific human experience and therefore thought worthy of bearing a name – Gully of Little Bran's Lad, Meadow of the Dead Goose. My map names not only every hillock, hollow, field, and cove, but also every private home and shop. This is the product of

5,000 years of human habitation, of course, but also reflects a way of seeing and valuing.

These many names are a testimony to the human scale of life on Iona. As the scale of physical size diminishes as one travels to the island–England, Scotland, Mull, Iona–the scale of individual and spiritual significance rises. Walking is the maximum desirable speed for seeing things fully enough to name them. And when we name things then we begin to value them. No wonder that we all want to be named and known.

Jayne and I walk out of our cottage to explore some of the beaches and coves on the west side of the island. The nearest beach lines the Bay at the Back of the Ocean. The name bespeaks a kind of familiarity and confidence in suggesting that a vast ocean has a back door. It brings the Atlantic down to a manageable size.

We are just beyond the driveway when I see a small but steep grassy mound perhaps ten feet high in the field by the side of the road. The map tells me it is Cnoc nan Aingeal– Hill of Angels. And of course there is a story attached.

Columba went out one day, having given strict instructions to the other monks that he wanted to be alone. But out of curiosity one of the monks secretly followed him and watched from a distance as Columba climbed up a small knoll and began to pray. The monk, Adomnan tells us, looked on in amazement as suddenly "holy angels, the citizens of the heavenly kingdom, were flying down with amazing speed, dressed in white robes, and began to gather around the holy man as he prayed."

I like that this place–known for centuries as the Hill

of Angels (and before that as a fairy mound)—is in Mrs. MacCormick's field, where the sheep are lambing. I like that Jayne can walk over and climb it herself for a picture or a prayer. I like that there is no memorial chapel here, no Celtic cross, no souvenir stand, not even a simple plaque or sign. It is a bump in a sheep pasture—and a place where angels once came down.

chapter two

Looking for the Holy–Discovered or Created?

We look more and more, but see less and less.
Phil Cousineau

Pilgrims are poets who create by taking journeys.
Richard R. Niebuhr

We determine to go that first evening to the service at the Abbey. It was built in the thirteenth century on the site of Columba's original wooden church by the Benedictines, those representatives of Roman Christianity who won the ecclesiastical struggle with a more Celtic-flavored Christianity in England in the seventh century. The Abbey eventually fell into ruins, but was restored throughout the twentieth century and now is the center of a flourishing religious community.

Walking to the church, we pass the ancient graveyard called Reilig Odhrain, the reputed burial place of forty-eight or more kings of Scotland, Ireland, and Norway, including Macbeth and Duncan, though none of this can be verified. In the past, when tourists asked which were the graves of Macbeth and Duncan, they were sometimes told that the ghosts of the two had argued so much that the locals had separated their graves and their locations now were lost.

The evening service is quiet and unexceptional, as it should be. The people of the community disappear quickly once it is over, so the seven of us wander separately within and around the church for an hour or so. The posters and pamphlets in the sanctuary and off the cloister remind me of the exhortations to righteousness one might find in the student union at a typical university: preserve the environment, be nice to animals, oppose war, and celebrate sexual diversity.

A cross made of two sticks leans in a corner of one of the transepts. Pinned on it are handwritten prayer requests: "Please pray for wee Malcolm," "Pray for a son and a brother," "For two young men killed in a car wreck." I find these engaging in a way that the exhortations and photographs on the posters are not. They put me in mind of Eliot's poem about his own spring pilgrimage in 1936 to Little Gidding, a site near Cambridge where Nicholas, John, and Susanna Ferrar had founded a religious community in the early seventeenth century. Eliot knew all about the tangle of motives that we bring to sacred places, including his own, and he sought to cut through them to what was important. The only legitimate goal for his brief pilgrimage, he concluded, was "to kneel/ Where prayer had been valid." One hopes that prayer is still valid on Iona, and so I say a short prayer for wee Malcolm.

When I step outside the church, Jayne beckons me over

to a circular wall of stones with a wooden covering sitting just outside the main door. "This is Columba's cell," she whispers, and I can tell that she is moved by seeing it, as she often is by places associated with devout people who have dedicated their lives to faith. I look at it for a minute and find that it doesn't do much for me, as these places usually do not.

I wander over and sit on a pleasant grassy knoll nearby. In a few minutes Jayne comes over with a smile on her face. "That wasn't Columba's cell," she laughs. "It's the well." Turns out the likely site of his cell is right next to me here on the grassy knoll called Tor Abba.

This raises a very old question. Do we experience the sacredness of a place, or do we experience merely our desire that a place be sacred? And does it matter whether a place is truly sacred or we only think it is? In Jayne's case, for instance, her misidentification of a holy site elicits in her a feeling of awe and respect for Columba's devotion, a feeling that may prompt her to aspire to the same. Does the mistake render the feeling, and subsequent action, invalid?

This is a specific case of a larger question. Do we *perceive* a reality that is outside us or do we *create* a reality inside our minds—or both? The English Romantic poets—some of whom came to Iona in the early nineteenth century—wrestled mightily with the question and influenced how we think about it today. Sometimes they talked as if the power that shaped reality was outside themselves in the natural world, to be perceived by the properly tuned mind and heart. Other times they spoke like Coleridge, who in the midst of despair wrote, "we receive but what we give" and "I may not hope from outward forms to win/ The passion and the life, whose fountains are within." Then again, Wordsworth thought it a mixture of the inner and the outer:

> *Therefore am I still*
> *A lover ... of all the mighty world*
> *Of eye, and ear,—both what they half create,*
> *And what perceive.*

Is there anything objectively sacred or transcendent about a place like Iona, or do we merely project our inner desires? Maybe Samuel Johnson was hinting at this issue when he visited in 1773 and reflected on the claim that it was the burial site of so many long-forgotten kings: "If he loves to sooth his imagination ... let him listen in submissive silence; for if he asks any questions, his delight is at an end." Johnson advises not pressing too hard on unverifiable claims. But we live in a more skeptical age and we insist on asking questions.

Is Iona a holy place? Yes, it is a "thin place" where the gap between this world and the transcendent world is easily crossed.

Is Iona a holy place? No, it is a place composed largely of Lewisian granite, some of the oldest rock in the world. It once was covered with oak, ash, birch, willow, and hazel, but now is almost treeless. It supports approximately eighty different species of birds. Just under 100 people live there permanently, mostly farming and tending to tourists.

Is Iona a holy place? Yes and no. It is not holy in itself, but it can be if you bring holiness with you.

Is Iona a holy place? I don't know. Hundreds of thousands of people come each year to visit. Many of them report finding themselves changed by the journey, though not many can say exactly how.

There is nothing of eternal significance on Iona that you cannot find on your own back porch, or within your own heart. But then again, I now understand why my colleague in California said his students looked back across the sound at the island and didn't want to leave. The locals report that some people come to Iona and hug the rocks. People also build small mounds of stone to leave behind. The beach where Columba is thought first to have landed is covered with them, built by passing visitors over many, many years.

It is not hard to figure out why. Leaving something behind is a fundamental human impulse that is the basis for all civilization. Today I am here; tomorrow I will be gone. I want to leave something behind to show that I existed. From this simple need we get pyramids and palaces, paintings and poems. And rock cairns in Columba's Bay.

✢ ✢ ✢

It's good that many people find Iona a sacred place. There aren't many holy places left in the world, and we need them as least as much as we need spotted owls and whales. Annie Dillard points out in "Teaching a Stone to Talk" that holy places have been disappearing rapidly since the Enlightenment and that we're the worse for it. "God used to rage at the Israelites for frequenting sacred groves. I wish I could find one.… Now we are no longer primitive; now the whole world seems not-holy."

But valuing the holy and knowing exactly what it is are not the same thing. People get mystical when they describe it precisely because words and categories fail. That doesn't make the holy unreal, only inexpressible. The best we can do is look for clues.

One clue is in the meaning of the word itself. Holy, as we have seen, means set apart—set apart because the holy is *extra*-ordinary, not of the everyday, even if it can and should be found in the everyday. Set apart also because the holy is dangerous, as seen in the boundary set around Sinai, and in the stern warnings regarding who can go into the Tabernacle's Holy of Holies—and what they must and must not do to come out alive.

This set apartness can be seen in the ground around the Iona Abbey even today. There are remains of what is called the vallum, a low mound of earth and ditch that runs around monastic sites in many places. At the Iona Abbey it encloses about twenty acres. It was not a place of defense against physical attackers, rather an announcement of intent to spiritual attackers.

The Celtic monks saw themselves as warriors for God and for good. They fought on behalf of the rest of the world against powers and principalities. The extremity of their discipline—prayer, fasting, Scripture memorization, and meditation—was to prepare them for spiritual warfare, just as a solider trains for battle. The vallum was a line drawn in the sand that said goodness prevails inside this space. This space is holy—it is set apart. Come here for help and healing and worship, or come not at all.

✛ ✛ ✛

In the end, it's not important to me to decide whether Iona is a holy place or not. I'm something of a tough sell when it comes to shrines and sacred places. My first spiritual instructors were inheritors of the religion of Oliver Cromwell, whose soldiers stabled their horses in Canterbury Cathedral and rode down the aisles breaking out the stained glass windows with their lances. So I have come to Iona with low expectations, which I think might be helpful.

I decided in advance that I would neither expect nor resist any spiritual resonances Iona might have. Samuel Johnson said at the time of his visit, "That man is little to be envied, whose patriotism would not gain force upon the plain of Marathon, or whose piety would not grow warmer among the ruins of Iona." But I can't help but feel that, even as he said this, Johnson was more concerned with creating a nice turn of phrase than he was with being more pious.

R. S. Thomas, the twentieth-century Welsh poet, seems closer to my own frame of mind in a poem about a small church in another remote Celtic place:

I often call there.
There are no poems in it
for me.

I, too, come to Iona doubting that there are any poems, or holy experiences, in it for me.

In fact, I discover this poem in a book of Thomas's collected poems that I buy in the Iona Abbey bookshop. It is one of a half dozen books I buy that day. At every holy site

I visit over the next two months, I buy books. I'm not sure whether I want the books to increase my chances of experiencing the holy, or more likely, as insulation against it.

There is something about expertise that kills experience. I know this is a very romantic and dubious notion–that analysis is the enemy of emotion–but there's something to it. Mark Twain remarked how much beauty and mystery he found in the Mississippi River until he trained to be a river-boat pilot. After that, every ripple and crosscurrent merely sent him a practical message about how to steer the boat.

I think the same may be true of expertise regarding sacred things, and so I am happy to have known very little about Celtic Christianity when I came to England. But I can't resist the books. And so I learn a little more everyday–not enough to be genuinely knowledgeable, but enough to feed my spiritual imagination. And the history of Celtic Christianity cooperates by having so very few hard facts and so much room for the imagination.

And so I walk around Iona without requiring anything of it, perhaps in hopes that it will require nothing of me. The sheep can simply be sheep, the rocks just rocks–harshly beautiful but not crying out for a hug. Columba's Hill of Angels does not have to call down angels for me; the sunset behind it will do just fine. I find myself understanding Mrs. MacCormick when Jayne questions her about whether she ever attends the services of the re-established Christian community at the Abbey. She pauses briefly and then says, diplomatically, "We're very busy."

Yes, I am willing for Iona to be simply a small island with a long history. But it won't let me off quite that easily. Neither does the small church in Thomas's poem. He remarks that services there are few now, and little goes on behind the altar screen. He claims that, unlike in biblical times when an encounter with God could be blinding, "I keep my eyes/ open and am not dazzled." But then in his explanation for why he is not dazzled, Thomas sets a hook in the reader that I feel bite into my jaw as I read the poem in the Abbey bookstore:

so delicately does the light enter
my soul from the serene presence
that waits for me till I come next.

This obscure and disappearing church, which has few services and no poems for the poet (except, of course, this poem he has now written), and little if any mystery left, has nonetheless this "serene presence" that patiently waits for him.

Does a phrase like "serene presence" betray our timidity in the modern world to invoke the name of God–for fear of mockery or misunderstanding–or is it an appropriate recognition that often all we hear is a "still, small voice" that is difficult to distinguish from the wind? Or does Thomas have something else in mind altogether?

Whatever it is, I realize that "serene presence" describes fairly well my experience of Iona. It is a place that makes me slow down–down to a walk. It is a place that invites me to reflect–on why I am here (on Iona and on this planet), on who was here before me and what they were up to, and on what I am supposed to learn from them about God and the sacred. But if I don't wish to reflect, or am not capable of reflection–or if I reflect and arrive at no particular con-

49

clusion – then Iona is content to be, for me, just another pleasant place.

✝ ✝ ✝

If I learn anything on Columba's island, it is something that I already know but need to learn again. It is that holiness, for all the talk of vallums and being set apart, must also get its hands dirty. The Celtic vision of life was synthetic and fluid more than analytic and categorical. They did not neatly separate natural and supernatural, secular and sacred, the functional and the artistic, the material and the spiritual. One thing flowed into another as streams flow into rivers and rivers flow into the sea.

The sacred, they insisted, must be integrated into the mundane, and the mundane into the sacred. When we first arrive on Iona, my son Matthew is disappointed to find houses and shops and farms. He had been expecting a place even smaller than the 2,000 acres of the island, with nothing but the remains of an earlier time.

I, on the other hand, am glad that Iona is a place where the normal activities of life go on, often with little thought of the religious community beyond the village. I like looking out our cottage window and seeing Mr. MacCormick walking across his small field holding in each hand a newborn lamb by the forelegs, the mother walking behind. I like that he and Mrs. MacCormick are "very busy."

I also like that Iona, the holy island, has a golf course. Most of the year it is a sheep pasture called the machair, a former beach that rose up thousands of years ago when the weight of the last ice age melted away. The monks raised barley there and now it is a common pasture by the Bay at the Back of the Ocean. You don't notice the golf holes, there being no distinction between fairway and green, unless you happen by one of them and spot the metal pin leaning precariously out. Columba of course knew nothing of golf, but I like to think that his understanding of grace persists in the scoring system used during the annual tournament in August—you play all eleven holes on the course, but only count your score on the best nine.

Farm next to Abbey, Hill of Angels next to golf course, abandoned marble works next to bay full of memorial cairns, holy man running to church to pray for young woman in labor—all this is as it must be if the holy is to be real for us, and if we are to be present to the holy. This is something that artists, for one, understand—as we were to discover.

While we are in Iona there is a major show in London at the National Gallery entitled "Seeing Salvation," a survey of depictions of Christ throughout European art history. Later I see it with my son Nate and am struck by a painting entitled "Christ carrying the Cross" by the twentieth-century British artist Stanley Spencer. Christ is depicted carrying the cross through the streets of Cookham, Spencer's small, native village. What strikes me is that almost no one in the crowded street is looking at him. All are going about their business, including two workmen following behind Christ carrying ladders that intersect each other in a way that mirrors Christ's cross.

Spencer believed that the Incarnation—God joining us—imparts to human life and everyday human activities a great dignity. It makes it possible to see common tasks as holy. In fact, Spencer depicts Christ as he does—walking through the streets of an ordinary English village with his cross, like the workmen with their ladders—to show, as the catalogue says, that "sacrificial loving is daily work, and joyful work at that." Jesus is just doing his job (or *the* job, as Spencer insists), the thing he came to do, and Spencer refuses to see that in mournful terms.

I think Columba might have agreed. I am sure he would have agreed with Spencer's description of his epiphany about the interpenetration of the holy and the mundane: "Quite suddenly I became aware that everything was full of special meaning and this made everything holy. The instinct of Moses to take his shoes off when he saw the burning bush was similar to my feelings. I saw many burning bushes in Cookham. I observed this sacred quality in the most unexpected quarters." And so did the Celts long before him.

This sense that the holy is all around us undercuts my ongoing attempts to keep it at arm's length—in a separate category that renders it unattainable (and therefore irrelevant). The single most effective way to deflect the impact others might have on our lives is to assign them to a category to which we do not ourselves belong. In this case, the category can be high—they are holy, saints, miracle workers, spiritual giants—or low—they are fools, gullible, out of touch, extremists. Either way, we are safe from them and the challenge of their lives. They are not like us, so we cannot fairly be expected to be like them. It's easy to pass off as humility what is actually laziness and self-indulgence, saying that holiness is beyond me – literally *unreal*-istic – something for better people to pursue. That attitude, in Spencer's terms, is a refusal to do your job.

Columba and the others were simply doing their job as they saw it. They were not trying to escape this world to reach the holy. They were trying to bring the holy into the world, a much different thing. More precisely still, and this is what separates them from other strains of Christianity that see the world primarily as a cesspool, they were trying to bring *out* the holiness that they perceived as already present in God's world. Even their acts of penance, so excessive seeming to us, were less acts of self-punishment than acts designed to replace an evil with a good, and thereby to cooperate with God in completing his creation.

✦ ✦ ✦

One of the most attractive aspects of Celtic Christianity is its stress on the importance of finding a soul friend – a notion that combines kindred spirit, mentor, spiritual director, confessor, and boon companion. The Celts called such a person an anachmara – a friend of the soul – and thought no one was complete – or safe – without one. The oft-repeated saying was that a person without a soul friend is like a body without a head. Such a friend does not merely make your life more pleasant, he or she makes your life more possible.

A soul friend could be someone your own age, but more often was an older person who acted as mentor and guide. Some of the great saints were soul friends to each other. One of the early tasks of a novice monk was to seek out a soul friend, usually from among one of the older monks. That senior monk would serve not only the various spiritual roles but also act as teacher, encourager, and friend, and had more authority over the life of his charge than did the abbot.

That authority was demonstrated in the right and responsibility of one soul friend to assign penance to the other for sins. This is something we do not readily understand. If the idea of a soul friend is one of the most attractive aspects of Celtic Christianity, their enthusiasm for penance is one of the things we moderns least understand or sympathize with. And yet the two are related.

We are attracted to the idea of soul friends because each of us has a profound desire to be known, to be valued, and to be guided (even protected). These things are as rare as they are desirable. How many people really know you? To how many people can you tell anything, including shameful things, with confidence that you will be better for it and their love for you will be undiminished? How many people are willing to put themselves at risk to help you?

And there *is* risk in a soul friendship. One monk assigned penance to another because he cared for him enough to want him to be holy. But he also did it out of fear for his own soul. The Celtic Christians believed that if a spiritual mentor did not deal adequately with a sin in his friend, the guilt of that sin fell on the mentor. Does anyone believe this today? Could our churches genuinely discipline their members and survive?

When we hear of the idea of soul friends, we all think we want one. I'm not so sure we do. We want someone to know, value, and guide us, but, at the same time, we do not want anyone telling us what to do. We are thoroughly modern and western—that is, we prize our individuality and autonomy. Our culture's great boast is "I did it my way." Or, slightly more belligerently, but amounting to the same thing, "Nobody tells *me* what to do!"

If you don't want anyone telling you what to do, then you are not ready for a soul friend. Telling you what to do is exactly what soul friends do. It is not because they are smarter or even more devout. It is because God has given them this job, and the necessary wisdom to carry it out. He or she may not be the person you like or respect the most, which is why you should not *pick* a soul friend. You should pray to have your soul friend revealed to you—and pray that the same would be revealed to the friend.

Soul friendships were maintained over great distances. Monks would often train at one monastery and then leave to join another or start one of their own. They would write to each other or even make long journeys. When Finnian of Clonard intuited that his soul friend Ciaran was dying at Clonmacnois, he traveled there because, as his hagiographer explained, "it was with him he studied his psalms and every kind of learning he had."

The Celts sometimes spoke as if soul friendship even transcended time. Patrick and Brigid were portrayed as friends even though Patrick died when she was a child and there is no evidence they ever met. Which raises the possibility that Patrick or Brigid or any of these saints can be a soul friend to me, these many centuries later—someone to teach, mentor, admonish, and guide.

If holiness was the job of these Celtic monks, then almost everything they did was supposed to be done with an attitude appropriate to holiness. That included copying books. Nothing in the thousand years between the fall of Rome and the rise of the Renaissance did more to preserve and extend western civilization than the monkish love of books. Every monastery that could afford it devoted an important amount of its time and resources to collecting, writing, and copying. Columba is said to have copied three hundred books himself.

We are too spoiled by copying machines and printing presses to easily understand what the hand copying of books entailed and signified. It required the stretching and scraping and treating of animal skins (one calfskin forming two folio pages); the collection of plants and tedious preparation of inks and paints; long hours of ruling and copying, and then more hours of proofing and correcting. Extensively illuminated books took even longer. The end result of months, sometimes years, of work was one copy of one book.

The book they copied the most, of course, was the Bible. And because they loved it, they could not be satisfied with merely copying it. They had to make it into a work of art.

The most famous artifact of Iona, and one of the great treasures of Celtic civilization, is the *Book of Kells*. Begun on Iona, some claim by Columba, but much more likely by his followers around 800, and possibly completed in Ireland, the *Book of Kells* is an illuminated and luminous manuscript of the gospels in Latin. More than that, however, it is an offering of love and devotion, and a tour de force of skill, creativity, and almost wild inventiveness. In the twelfth century, Giraldus Cambrensis described it as aptly as any: "Fine craftsmanship is all about you, but you might not notice it. Look more keenly at it, and you will penetrate to the very shrine of art. You will make out intricacies, so delicate and subtle, so exact and compact, so full of knots and links, with colors so fresh and vivid, that you might say that all this was the work of an angel, and not of man."

But it is because it is the work of men and not of angels that it is so amazing—work done through Scottish winters, in cold and gloom, under threat of attack by Viking raiders, by a handful of believers on a tiny island, in a society hard pressed simply to meet the elemental needs of food and shelter. The creation of the *Book of Kells* is an extremist act if ever there was one.

The book totals 340 pages, 33 of which have major decorations, and only two of which have no decoration at all. It required about 185 calfskins for its vellum pages, an indication of the prosperity of the monastery at the time. Though scripted and illuminated by as few as seven monks on the edge of the civilized world, it is literally an international work. The text used is Jerome's fourth-century Latin Vulgate, a work begun in Rome and completed in Bethlehem. The pigments used for the various colors arrived in Iona from all parts of the world—the yellow arsenic from Italy, Hungary, Macedonia or beyond; the blue from Asian indigo or northern European woad; one version of red from a Mediterranean insect; and, most precious of all, the deep, cobalt blue from lapis lazuli, found at the time only in a single mine in northern Afghanistan.

Each page, whether of text or design, was meticulously laid out using compasses, rulers, knives, straight edges, and templates. Approximately 2,000 lines of text begin with an ornamental letter, each one a unique shape (often of an animal) and color. This device not only infuses the book with small, bright explosions of creativity and color, it also allows readers to find particular passages more quickly (as in, one can imagine, "Read from the wolf to the peacock").

The *Book of Kells* has the human smell all over it. Along with its breath-taking intricacies are numerous mistakes, especially in the copying of text. Mistakes caught in time were scrapped off, but other incorrect words have dots between the letters or around the words to cancel them. One page was accidentally copied twice.

A few of the seeming lapses may even be a theological statement. The elaborate page depicting Christ has two places in the upper corners that have been prepared to be filled in, like every other square nanometer of such pages, but are curiously blank. Some have suggested this was done intentionally to express humility and an awareness of human fallenness.

The scribes, in fact, seemed comfortable with finitude and human limitations. One page has a hole that occurred during the elaborate processing of the calfskin vellum. Rather than reject the piece, the scribe simply copied around it, an indication of a willingness to work with whatever life presents (and a testament to how expensive vellum was).

In the same vein, one finds touches of humanity and humor that draw us to the Celts. The most famous page of the manuscript, arguably the most complex execution of calligraphy and illumination ever, is the Chi-Rho page from the beginning of the Gospel of Matthew. Tucked in a corner at the bottom of the large X-shaped *chi* is a tiny scene sprung from the imagination of a master craftsman. Two mice are nibbling on opposite sides of a communion wafer. Behind each mouse hunches a cat, and on the back of each cat sits another mouse.

Some scholars interpret the scene as an allusion to those Christians who partake of communion unworthily. Others suggest it may be a complicated theological joke having to do with the doctrine of transubstantiation–if the bread of communion becomes the actual body of Christ, are the mice that eat the wafer ingesting Christ himself, perhaps to be ingested in turn by the observing cats? Holy mice? Holy cats?

Whatever the explanation, I like thinking about the fellow who did it. Having worked in concert with others on this one page for days or weeks, he decides that holiness and devotion are not incompatible with a smile and a nod to everyday life. So he buries his little witticism there at the foot of the name of Christ at the very opening of the gospels, to be absorbed by the larger design of which it is a part, just as our individual lives are a small but significant detail in the overall design of creation. Yet there it is for the patient, discerning eye to see, and when one does see it, one joins with Giraldus in saying, "The oftener I see the book, and the more carefully I study it, the more I am lost in ever fresh amazement."

Not everyone over the centuries has been as amazed by the *Book of Kells* as they should have been. In the eleventh and twelfth centuries, long after it had been transferred from Iona to Kells in Ireland, blank spaces on some pages were used to record property transactions, sort of like writing a grocery list on an original copy of the Magna Carta. In the fifteenth century someone used a blank page to copy a poem complaining about church taxation. In the next century, one Gerald Plunket wrote numerous annotations on the pages and graced the manuscript with his initials and signatures. In the nineteenth century the pages were butchered by an obtuse vandal who gilded the edges and chopped them to a more convenient size for binding. In 1849 Queen Victoria carried the arrogance of "the royal 'we'" to a new height by joining Gerald Plunkett and signing the book (or so she thought) with her royal signature. We are not amused.

Perhaps this is instructive. What is holy to me may be ho-hum to you, and vice versa. The sacred does not insist on its sacredness. It is there to be experienced – or not. It is essentially shy. It is patient, not demanding. We can seek it out, reverence it, turn our lives toward it, or we can walk right past, preoccupied with our own affairs.

✠ ✠ ✠

I buy a small volume on the *Book of Kells* in the Abbey bookstore, and a number of other books. One purports to collect the wisdom of Columba and another is a book of Celtic blessings. Scholars will tell you that very little can be tied reliably to Columba himself, the rest being the product of a Columba industry that started in his own lifetime and has continued to the present day.

One hymn that many consider authentically from his hand strikes a chord of genuine humility and self-understanding that I find powerful even standing in the store:

> *I beg that me, a little man*
> *trembling and most wretched*
> *rowing through the infinite storm of this age,*
> *Christ may draw after Him to the lofty*
> *most beautiful haven of life.*

Columba knew what it was to row through a storm at sea in a small, animal skin boat. And he knew that its terrors, however great, were small compared to the spiritual and psychological terrors of "rowing through the infinite storm of this age"—a storm we still feel blowing.

If we can indeed have soul friends across time, then I may have found one. Some of the writing attributed to Columba or those in his circle awakens a feeling of affinity despite the gap of centuries. I read "Shame on my thoughts, how they stray from me! I fear great danger from this on the Day of Eternal Judgment" and I think the writer has been inside my own mind. "They run, they distract, they misbehave before the eyes of the great God. … One moment they follow the ways of loveliness, and the next the ways of riotous shame!"

And yet we should not think Columba all anxiety and self-abasement. There is a strong element of blessing and gratitude that runs throughout everything associated with him and with Celtic Christianity generally. "Behold Iona!"

he declares, "A blessing on each eye that seeth it." He and others bless each day ("This day is your love-gift to me. This dawn … I take if from your hand"), the seasons ("Autumn is a good time for visiting"), the home ("A blessing upon your new dwelling,/ Upon your newly-kindled fire"), the people and animals whose paths he crosses, and even, in one of Adomnan's stories, the cart in which he is to ride.

This sense of blessing and gratitude could not be further from our own culture of unfulfillable desire. From Declaration of Independence to economic system to human-potential and psychotherapeutic movements, we pursue happiness and fulfillment and the satiation of our desires—and, at the end of the day, we are not satisfied. We must not, in fact, be satisfied, or the mad race would come grinding to a halt, and what would we do then?

The Celtic Christians understood this. One poem begins "Many a time I wish I were other than I am." It speaks of the universal longing for escape from "the weight of duty." And, then, in a telling phrase, it begs God to "set me free from the lordship of desire." How can we, who live in a culture that multiplies desires and then calls them needs and rights, ever hope to be freed from the tyranny of insatiable wanting? The poem answers this question in a way that captures much of what attracts us to these ancient seekers:

> *Help me to find my happiness*
> *in acceptance of my purpose;*
> *in friendly eyes;*
> *in work well done;*
> *in quietness born of trust;*
> *and, most of all,*

in the awareness of your presence
in my spirit.

This represents a spiritual economy founded in simplicity and practical wisdom. It saturates daily life with spiritual significance, hence the endless prayers and blessing for every human activity: lighting the morning fire, making bread, working in the fields, setting out on a journey, banking the fire at evening's end, and, perhaps most needful of all, sleeping safely through the night.

Much of this is rooted in the need to feel secure in a dangerous world. But also running throughout Celtic spirituality is an emphasis on right priorities—most important things first—that gives us clues to the underlying logic of practices such as Columba's fasting: "May no morsel of my body's partaking/ Add to my soul's freight." This is in the spirit of "if thy eye offend thee, pluck it out," a purposefully shocking biblical hyperbole designed to explode complacency and set us thinking on first things.

Columba combined in this life simple devotion and faithfulness in everyday things with heroic spiritual combat against personal and cosmic evil. Reflect on the eulogy for Columba written at his death, and wish such a one for yourself:

> ... *he kept watch while he lived* ...
> *no fog of drink, nor fog of delights—*
> *he avoided the fill of his mouth....*
> *He was full of light.*
> *He was an ample fort for the stranger* ...
> *He was a shelter for the naked,*
> *he was a teat to the poor* ...

> *He destroyed the darkness of envy,*
> *he destroyed the darkness of jealousy ...*
> *What he conceived keeping vigil,*
> *by action he attained.*

May we, likewise, find our way out of the fog. May we be full of light. May we act to bring into reality the world we conceive of in our hearts.

✝ ✝ ✝

We spend only two nights on Iona. As the sun sets before the last one, Jayne and I walk over to the Bay at the Back of the Ocean again to watch it go down into the Atlantic. It is a different beauty than the *Book of Kells*, but both remind me of another danger, one as insidious as trying to live off other people's spiritual experience. It is the danger of confusing the truly sacred with the merely aesthetic.

I say *merely* not because the aesthetic is not one of God's greatest gifts, but because it is, nonetheless, so much less than God's ultimate gift. It has become a tradition at tropical resorts all over the world to gather at the beach and watch the sun go down and to applaud at the moment it disappears under the horizon. It is a well-meaning impulse, but for most who do so it is unconscious idol worship. There is an aesthetic dimension to the sacred, and there can be a sacred dimension to the aesthetic, but they are not, in fact, the same thing.

Many want to turn Columba, Iona—and Celtic Christianity generally—into aesthetic and ethical fodder: a feel good experience that celebrates nature, poetry, kindheartedness, egalitarianism, and the like. All of this can be found—in the stories at least, if not in verifiable history—but this is not the true stuff of the sacred, or at least not the sufficient stuff. Aesthetic moments and ethical content can be created out of our own guts. (We, after all, are the ones who decide that a sunset is beautiful.) But Columba and those like him did not climb into their boats and trust themselves to the sea simply to find what they could manufacture for themselves. They believed in and were looking to make evident in the world a true transcendence that breaks the glass ceiling of the merely temporal, a transcendence on which the sacred finally depends. If we are going to claim them as examples and guides, we shouldn't seek for anything less.

chapter three

To Lindisfarne – A Sometimes Island

What is best for the Christian life? Simplicity and single-mindedness.
Colman, a student of Columba

A saint is one who exaggerates what the world neglects.
G.K. Chesterton

We leave Iona early in the morning. The ferry schedule had said that if you wanted the early ferry back to Mull, you had to contact the ferry office in Tobermoray. I had told the ticket taker on the ferry coming over that we needed an early crossing two days later and asked if I should call the office. "You've told me," he had replied, "and that's all you need to do." Yes, Iona is a small place.

I am not unhappy to leave Iona, but I know I must come back. This is only the first site on our unintended pilgrimage, and we have lashed ourselves to a schedule. We load back into the Space Cruiser. The next stop is across Scotland into northeast England to another island called Lindisfarne.

This is a journey the monks of Iona made themselves. Within forty years after Columba's death in 597, they were asked by the Christian king of Northumbria to evangelize his kingdom. King Oswald had lived on Iona as a boy while in exile, and when he gained his throne, he asked for a monk to teach his subjects about God, one of many examples of Celtic missionaries taking their understanding of the faith to a non-Celtic people.

The first man sent failed in his mission and blamed it on the people. He returned to Iona and pronounced them "too obstinate and barbarous in temperament to learn the Christian faith." When he gave this report, another monk, Aidan, stood up and said that perhaps the man had been too severe, and that the people needed to learn "the milk of simple teaching" before they were given "the strong meat of Christian doctrine." Aidan then learned what many have discovered since: Speak up in a meeting and you may be given work to do. He was sent the next day to Northumbria, where he served for the rest of his life.

It takes us all day to get from Iona to Lindisfarne. Halfway there I notice the Space Cruiser is overheating and recall the earlier mutterings about the lousy design of the Toyota cooling system. I use all the tricks learned from a lifetime of driving old cars, including turning the heater on full blast to draw heat from the engine. Eventually we stop for repairs in Edinburgh, not wanting to melt down in some remote spot between sacred places.

As I sit on the curb waiting for the mechanic to arrive, I think of Eliot's attempt to cut through Christmas-time idealizing of the Magi's trip to Bethlehem. He imagines the camel drivers cursing and complaining, but worst of all were "the voices singing in our ears, saying/ That this was all folly." Perhaps the modern suspicion that this is all folly—not just the pilgrimage but the whole venture of faith—is the biggest burden the self-conscious pilgrim has to carry these days.

At any rate, the repairs are only partially successful, and by the time we arrive in the night at Lindisfarne, the Space Cruiser is bubbling and steaming like a primitive locomotive.

✠ ✠ ✠

Aidan was given Lindisfarne from which to establish his mission in 635. It was and still is a tidal island, cut off twice a day from the mainland as the sea covers the road. The ninth-century poet Aethelwulf describes it as a place "where the waves are eager to curl over the shore with grey water, but rush to lay them bare as they go to their backward course, and the blue depths encircle a sacred land."

There is something evocative about this place that both is and is not an island. The source of much of our information about the evangelizing of Britain, including the story above of Aidan's first coming to Lindisfarne, is Bede, England's first great historian, who wrote in the eighth century. Bede's poetic description of Lindisfarne suggests something about the monastic life and the life of faith generally: "As the tide ebbs and flows, this place is surrounded twice daily by the waves of the sea like an island, and twice, when the sands are dry, it becomes again attached to the mainland." Isolation and connection, retreat and advance, solitude as preparation for engagement—from island to mainland and back twice a day—this is the rhythm of the spiritual life.

By all reports Aidan won over the pagans of Northumbria by the gentleness of his spirit and the consistency of his life. Oswald gave him a horse to ride around the kingdom, but Aidan gave it away to the first poor person he met. When Oswald chided him for giving away a fine horse, Aidan asked if Oswald thought the child of a mare more valuable than a child of God.

When rich people gave Aidan things, he would sell them to buy the freedom of slaves, many of whom joined him on Lindisfarne. Bede tells us Aidan openly reprimanded the rich and powerful when they did wrong, but rather than scold the peasants, "he much preferred to encourage people in the good they were doing." His method of evangelism was simply to walk around the countryside, talking with whoever crossed his path. Aidan chose to walk because it kept him on he same level as the people he met. One can't help but think the church had moved backward by the time a later archbishop insisted that all bishops ride horses to establish their dignity.

Aidan's last days were spent leaning against the buttresses of a small wooden church, meeting with anyone passing by who wanted to talk and pray. On the night Aidan died, Cuthbert, the most famous name associated with Lindisfarne, was a teenager guarding sheep in the fields. Bede tells us Cuthbert saw a ball of light ascending into the clouds. The next day he heard that Aidan had died and concluded that the light was Aidan's soul traveling to heaven. He decided to become a monk. Eventually Cuthbert became the head of the monastery at Lindisfarne and later bishop of Northumbria.

✛ ✛ ✛

Jayne and I pass by a statue of Aidan in the cemetery on the way to an early morning service on Lindisfarne at St. Mary the Virgin. There are twelve of us there for communion, a number Columba would have liked. The service is led by a woman, a middle-aged priest, attended by an older woman with gnarled hands. The church is small and we sit in the choir, looking across at each other. A man from Nottinghamshire is here for the week, and he plays beautiful music of his own composition on a pipe. He also sings, his gentle voice amplified by the stone walls.

This service marks a further step on my pilgrimage. Iona is more physically evocative for me than Lindisfarne, but this sharing of communion among a dozen believers on an early weekday morning has more spiritual resonance for me than I have felt in a long time. I begin to understand the monastic rationale for structuring the day around worship.

After the service I thank the man from Nottinghamshire and ask if he is a professional musician. He hesitates a moment, then says, "Well, I don't currently have work, so I make music." I want to say to him that I think by the Celtic understanding (and by Stanley Spencer's) he does have work, important work, and that he is doing it well.

✛ ✛ ✛

Cuthbert was not an immediate hit with the monks at Lindisfarne, saints apparently not always being recognizable at first sight. Bede tells us that when Cuthbert was sent to oversee the work, the monks openly insulted him. He responded with a cheerful graciousness that eventually wore out their spite. He also impressed them with his devotion, staying up three and four nights in a row for prayer and staving off sleepiness in the day by hard labor or visiting the sick.

✠ ✠ ✠

After the church service the tourist begins to win out over the pilgrim in my head. We have only the one night to spend on Lindisfarne, and I want to see Bamburgh Castle and Durham Cathedral and still get to Cambridge tonight. Because of the tide, we either have to leave by 10:30 in the morning or wait until early afternoon. I lean toward squeezing as much as we can in by 10:30 and then heading out. Jayne has more sense.

The friendly young woman who runs the pub and guesthouse where we stay lets me in on a local secret. She says the tide is extremely low at this time of the year and may not cover the road despite what the tide tables say. She takes me out of the guesthouse and points toward the small harbor. "Look between those two houses. See that rock in the bay? As long as you can see that rock you can get off the island. When it's covered, so is the road." I am delighted to find a physical marker that is superior to the abstraction of tables. I find myself wishing there were similarly tangible markers for the spiritual life. Perhaps there are.

Because we decide to stay longer, we take our children back to St. Mary the Virgin. I am reading the displays that give historical background when I hear singing. I look around to find my family, sitting in different parts of the otherwise empty church, spontaneously singing hymns. They sing a few verses of a song, then sit quietly until someone starts a new one. Julie, sitting alone up at the front with her back to the others, sings "I Surrender All" by herself. I know my wife is transported by this moment – it meets almost all her criteria for heaven – and I feel the blessing of it myself, though I do not join in. The display I have been reading says the part of the church where they are sitting is the most likely site of Aidan's original church, and I want to think he would be pleased.

✠ ✠ ✠

Perhaps the most famous story about Cuthbert underscores the common association of these holy men with animals. When he was prior of Melrose Abbey before coming to Lindisfarne, he used to get up in the middle of the night and go out to pray. One night another monk followed him and watched him go down to the river, wade into the water up his neck, and pray and sing psalms until dawn. When he came out of the river, two otters followed and curled around his feet, trying to warm him. After the sun had risen, Cuthbert blessed the otters and they returned to the river.

Why is getting along well with animals seen as a sign of holiness? Clearly it echoes numerous biblical stories – think Daniel's lions – and the Celtic storytellers linked their saints to the Bible whenever they could. Further, it suggests a repairing of the rifts caused by the Fall. If animals were at peace with each other and with humankind in Eden, then a person with whom even the wild animals were at peace was a person close to God.

✠ ✠ ✠

We walk around the harbor and the priory ruins, then look over the acre of rock a few yards off from the main part of Lindisfarne called Thrush Island, more popularly known as St. Cuthbert's Island. It's the place Cuthbert made a trial run at the solitary life, you might say, before heading farther out to sea to the more remote Farne Islands to fully explore the spiritual possibilities of isolation. It seems wise of him to have approached God in small steps. In the Bible, people who come into the presence of God tend to fall to the ground and put their face in the dirt. Given our affection these days for self-esteem, we like to think of a meeting with the Creator as something of a negotiation between interested parties.

Cuthbert thought otherwise. He sailed out to Farne to fast and pray and study precisely because he had some sense of the gulf between himself and God, but also, it is important to add, because he knew the gulf was much larger than it needed to be. I, on the other hand, want to pretend that the gulf between holiness and me is unspanable, so that no one will condemn me for being the spiritual sluggard I eagerly admit that I am.

Everything about the lives of these saints, and the many around them whose names have been lost, is an affront to modern sensibilities. They were ascetic where we are hedonistic, spiritual where we are materialistic, self-sacrificing where we are self-indulging, God-centered where we are self-centered, focused where we are diffuse, single in purpose where we are scattered, absolute where we are relativistic, open-handed where we are acquisitive, full of gratitude where we are full of complaint.

But if they affront us, they also call to us in a voice that we can still just recognize. We do not want to live their lives, but we want very much something they seemed to have had—something we can't quite put our finger on. Perhaps we want their clarity. They were clear in their minds and hearts about the ultimate purpose and meaning of life. They knew why they were alive and what they were to do with the short time they had. Amid all their striving they had a peace about things, an acceptance of the world and their place in it—and, paradoxically, a determination to change that world and themselves. They were forever blessing things and forever trying to make things better. They fit into their world in a way in which many of us do not quite fit into ours. In a word, they were content.

✛ ✛ ✛

These men—and women like Julian of Norwich—had a hunger for solitude that at times was almost ravenous. According to Bede, Cuthbert believed that the strength of a monk's youth should be spent in service to others, but that the reward for such service was solitude in later life. Late in his own life, Cuthbert made his move out to Farne. He built a circular cell and oratory out of rocks, peat, timber, and thatch. There he prayed, studied Scripture, sang, and did battle with the spiritual forces of evil.

Though it may seem paradoxical, this desire for solitude was parallel, not antithetical, to the call to community and service. We must realize that the life of solitude was an active life, and that it was in fact itself a service—to the community and to the world. It is a testimony to our own spiritual emaciation that we tend to think of a life of retreat as escapist, a kind of vacation from the clichéd real world. Instead, it was more often like being alone in the foxhole nearest enemy lines.

As much as Cuthbert may have been serving the world while alone on Farne Island, it was not the kind of service the world wanted from him. When in 684 a new bishop was needed for Northumberland, a group of churchmen sailed to Farne and asked Cuthbert to take the post. He refused. Then the king himself went to Cuthbert and begged him to accept the office, and he reluctantly agreed.

Cuthbert returned to face-to-face service to the people, traveling hundreds of miles in what is now northern England and southern Scotland. He was once again, as when a young monk, "sharing the conditions" of those he served, "directing their eyes toward heaven." This pregnant phrase of Bede's, "sharing the conditions," is full of wisdom. There can be no effective witness without "sharing the conditions." Likewise, there can be no building up of the body, no encouragement, no word of discipline, no believable word of hope, no transforming love without "sharing the conditions." When Aidan preferred to walk at eye level rather than ride the King's fine horse, he was sharing the conditions. When Columba rushed to the church to pray for the woman in labor, he was sharing the conditions.

Though I know that the conditions are more than physical, I can't help wondering whether, sitting at my computer in the suburbs, I am really sharing the conditions as they exist today. My conscience is not easy on this matter, and I am hungry for rationalizations. I wonder if I am not like Queen Victoria when her royal yacht stopped at Iona in 1847—a time when the islanders were near starvation because of the great potato famine. Prince Albert went ashore to inspect the monastery ruins, but the Queen records in her diary that she and the ladies stayed on the boat and sketched.

Cuthbert spent what time he had left to spend in two years of travel and service. Exhausted and knowing his life was near an end, he resigned his post and returned to Farne to spend his last days. Over the winter his brothers from Lindisfarne visited him and provided for his needs. He asked them to leave him alone for a while, however, and during a stormy period in March they were unable to sail to the island. When they finally came they found him near death, with only a few onions for food. He took his final communion and gave last instructions to those who loved him. He then, in the words of Bede, "raised his eyes towards heaven, and stretched out his arms as if to embrace his Savior. His gaunt face broke into a smile, and the breath went from his body."

As arranged beforehand, one of the monks waved two torches throughout the night from the highest point on the island, signaling to the others on Lindisfarne that Cuthbert had died. When those in the watchtower saw the signal, they immediately "rushed down to the church where the monks were already assembled. The monks spent the night giving thanks to God for Cuthbert's life on earth."

✛ ✛ ✛

It is past noon when we finish our walk around Lindisfarne. The tide charts say we can't get off the island, but a glance at the rock in the bay indicates the road is not yet covered. We hop in the Space Cruiser and drive over the still-dry causeway that connects Lindisfarne with the rest of the world.

I now can see clearly what I had seen only dimly in the dark of our arrival last night. There, a few hundred yards south of the paved road, are a series of tall wooden poles that have long shown the way for pilgrims who walk to Lindisfarne at low tide. They stretch out across the mud flats like spindly sentinels, evidence that sometimes the path to the sacred is clearly marked.

After a failed attempt to tour Bamburgh Castle, visible across the water from the island and site of Oswald's fortress, we head for Durham.

In coming to Durham we are following Cuthbert again. In his last days he acknowledged with irritation that his burial place was likely to become a shrine: "Although I am a sinner, many people foolishly regard me as a saint. So if I am buried at Lindisfarne, you will be flooded with visitors coming to my grave. And they will disturb the peace of the monastery." He was buried at Lindisfarne nonetheless, but later Viking raids and church politics led to his remains eventually ending up, after long wanderings, at Durham.

I have seen and admired many cathedrals on various continents, but Durham Cathedral instantly becomes my favorite. The variety of designs on its gigantic Romanesque columns – spirals, diamonds, vertical grooves, and zig-zags – makes them seem more playful than ponderous. The Cathedral's setting on the river Wear is so picturesque that it seems almost contrived.

When Cuthbert's body came to Durham, along with it came the magnificent *Lindisfarne Gospels*, an illuminated manuscript created near the beginning of the eighth century that is second only to the *Book of Kells* in this period. Completed as a homage to Cuthbert's memory within a few decades after his death, and close to a century before *Kells*, it anticipates many of the devices that the latter multiples to greater effect.

On the initial page of the Luke gospel alone there are more than 10,000 red dots, the simplest design element on the page. On the same page is another example of monastic wit. Running within the border along the right-hand margin is the elongated body of a cat. Its head is at the lower corner and it is eyeing a string of birds running along the border at the bottom of the page. It is a greedy cat, it seems, for it already has eight birds within its page-long body.

Cats must have been a common presence around monasteries. There are a few padding around the *Book of Kells*. And a favorite poem of Celtophiles expresses a monk scholar's humorous sense of kinship with his mouse-hunting cat:

> *He enjoys darting around,*
> *striving to stick his claw into a mouse;*

> *I am happy*
> *striving to grasp some complex idea.*

In the Celtic understanding, everything has its place in the divine scheme of things:

> *The task which he performs is the one*
> *for which he was created;*
> *and I am competent at my task,*
> *bringing darkness to the light.*

✛ ✛ ✛

In time a grand shrine to Cuthbert was constructed within the present Cathedral, becoming during the later Middle Ages one of the most popular pilgrimage sites in all of Britain, abetted by the report that when his casket was opened 400 years after his death, his body was still undecayed. The remains of the shrine still exist today behind the altar at the east end of the Cathedral.

The shrine was greatly reduced in splendor in 1540 during the English Reformation, but it is still too splendid for me. I tend to agree with Cuthbert's own view that calling him a saint doesn't do him or us much good. As a saint in a marble and gold tomb, he is a mildly interesting historical artifact—and as such not greatly different from his rough ivory comb preserved in the Cathedral Treasury. The Cuthbert who has a chance of affecting me is the man of faith who "shared the conditions" of the people he served.

I actually am more impressed to find that Bede is at Durham Cathedral as well. His tomb is at the opposite end of the Cathedral from Cuthbert, in the Galilee Chapel. Discovering for myself what any guidebook would have told me makes the discovery all the more delightful and moving. Though I have long known Bede as a name, I have in the few days of our travels come to have great affection for him as a person. In reading from his history of the English church, I feel his own affection for the men and women he admires and his disappointment with those who fail to love and serve. Bede's gentle and irenic spirit attracts and instructs me.

Both these qualities may derive from his own suffering. Bede was only seven when his parents sent him to be raised by a monk who was founding a new monastery. When about thirteen he was sent to another new monastery at Jarrow. Within a year it was devastated by a plague that killed everyone except the head of the monastery and Bede. Amazingly, the two of them—priest and boy—continued in the midst of death to perform the daily liturgies of worship, praying all the time for others to come to join them. What does this say to us who today are asked to measure the success of our churches by how fast they grow?

Perhaps I feel close to Bede because of his love of books and learning. As an adult he helped build what was likely the best library in Britain—and we should remember that monasteries generally were the heart of the intellectual and artistic and social world of the time, especially when we ask why anyone would want to be a monk. I hear the voice of a kindred spirit—a "soul friend"—when he says, "While I willingly submitted to all the rules of monastic life, and while I have attended all the services in the monastery church, my chief delight has always been in study, writing, and teaching." Which is to say, the rules were fine, the church services were important, but, ah, the books!

And so study and teach and write he did, including both a poetic and prose biography of Cuthbert, throughout a long and profitable life. And then he died as any scholar, especially any scholar of faith, would long to die, as a pupil of Bede's has recorded. In the spring of 735, Bede rushed to complete a translation of the Gospel of John into the vernacular language of the people before death would overtake him. One evening he sensed his end was near and insisted on dictating all night so that he might finish. At nine the next morning, one of the series of secretaries who was writing as he spoke urged him to take no further trouble and to rest. Bede replied, "It is no trouble. Go and sharpen your pen so you can write faster."

At noon he distributed to fellow monks the sum total of his earthly possessions, which included pepper, some linen, and incense. He asked them to pray for him and expressed his readiness for death: "It is now time for my soul to be set free from this decaying body. I have had a long life, during which God has blessed me greatly. But now I long to see Christ my King in the fullness of his beauty."

As dusk fell one of the young monks pointed out that the last sentence of the Gospel of John remained to be translated. Fittingly that sentence is about a world full of books. Bede dictated the translation and the young monk said, "It is finished." Bede echoed him, "It is well finished," and then asked to be lifted up so that he could take a final look at the place where he had spent so many years in prayer. Bede's pupil completes his description of the scene: "The young monk lifted Bede's head, and Bede chanted in a low whisper – 'Glory be to the Father, and to the Son, and to the Holy Spirit.' Then he breathed his last."

It is an old Roman idea that the goal of living is to prepare for a good death. The final test of wisdom about life is knowing how to think and act when confronted with its end. But surely this wisdom is best displayed over a lifetime, not just in the final hours. We are told Bede spent his final nights praying and singing psalms. "His arms were almost continually outstretched, in a posture of thankfulness to God. Indeed I can truthfully affirm that I have never known anyone so filled with gratitude as Bede."

Gratitude is the natural response to realizing that one has received better than one deserves. It is, in short, the appropriate response to grace. What a sobering admonishment to us who so readily complain. Bede, like those about whom he wrote, died well because he had lived well.

✢ ✢ ✢

We leave Durham after only a few hours because, like many modern pilgrims, we are in a hurry. We have a place we need to be and things the next day we need to do. Our time for collective pilgrimage is expired. Now it is time to return to what passes for real life.

As I drive the Space Cruiser in the night back south to Cambridge, I wonder what I know now that I didn't know a week ago. What have Iona and Lindisfarne and Durham taught me – or have I given them enough time to teach me anything? And what kind of learning is it likely to be anyway – of the head, of the heart, of the will?

Nearing Cambridge late at night, everyone quiet with

their tiredness and their thoughts, I notice the sign for the turnoff that leads to Little Gidding, the site of the seventeenth-century religious community that had come to my mind on Iona. Because they gave shelter for a night to a fleeing King Charles during the English Civil War, they were later ransacked and occupied by the victorious Parliamentary forces, ending a brave experiment in wedding work and worship. A new religious community was re-established there in the early twentieth century. I have taken students there myself in the past because of Eliot's poem about his own visit.

But tonight I am merely driving by on the highway and thinking about Little Gidding and what Eliot found there. I like that he mentions the pigsty in the poem, a reminder that sacred places are also and necessarily earthy places. I like that he is unsure of what to make of the visit:

> *And what you thought you came for*
> *Is only a shell, a husk of meaning....*

But I also like that though he is unsure, he still tries to capture meaning in words. He spends the whole poem mulling and probing and hazarding guesses as to what this place and its history and all that it symbolizes might mean—and also what his own coming might mean. I like it because ultimately holiness is only significant if it is personal.

Has this pilgrimage encouraged holiness in me? It's hard to say. I find I like Columba, and Aidan, and Cuthbert, and Bede—trolls and skeptical scholars notwithstanding. I like the stories about them—the mythical as well as the historical—and even that they often can't be told apart. It doesn't bother me that I may be creating realities in my head as much as perceiving them beyond my nose. After all, inside my head is where I live.

But liking these fellows and enjoying my visit to these islands is not the same as being changed by them. What do these long-dead, holy or not-so-holy men have to say to me? And no matter what they say, what are the chances that I will allow them to make a difference in my life?

I ponder these things as the Space Cruiser pulls into Cambridge in the early morning hours, spewing and wheezing to the last.

chapter four

From London to Dublin – Nibbling on the Sacred

Imagine there's no heaven,
It's easy if you try,
No hell below us,
Above us only sky …

John Lennon

He was despised and rejected by men;
a man of sorrows and acquainted with grief.

Isaiah 53:3

A pilgrimage is never finished. You go home, but you take some of the place and the experience with you. Shop dealers hope you take a souvenir. My wife inevitably brings back rocks. Most pilgrims are content, as on Iona, to build small memorial mounds of stones. Jayne takes the stones home with her. For my part, I take home from Iona my first wedding ring after twenty-eight years of marriage, but lose it a few weeks later.

But I also take away some still, small voices. These voices continue to whisper to me of increased possibilities for living. They whisper to me certain verbs–simplify, focus, release, risk, commit, pray, bless, believe. They whisper certain nouns–peace, gratitude, contentment, solitude, discipline, friendship, reverence. Most of all, they whisper that word which is both verb and noun, action and state of being–they whisper the word *love.* Love of creation, love of kindred spirits and of strangers, love of learning and wisdom and the imagination, love of home and of journey, love of peace and justice, love of prayer and worship. Love of all these things, but greatest love for the one who made them because of love for us.

As I continue to read the books I have collected throughout my pilgrimage, I read that we cannot reasonably credit any of these qualities to these Celtic saints and those who followed after them. The stories are too legendary or too derivative or too self-serving. They have been used and sometimes created by partisans for partisan ends to create a history that we wish for, not one that was. That's okay. Part of me is a post-modern man. I am looking for a story to belong to, not an airtight worldview to defend. And these stories, which for some reason no one bothered to tell me as a child, are some of the best I have heard–some of the best since I first heard the story that starts, "In the beginning God...."

I give storytellers the benefit of the doubt. I do not feel the need to prove that these stories happened; prove to me, if you think it worth the time, that they did not. The least that can be said with absolute confidence is that these men—and the women whose stories are less often recorded—were catalysts for remembered greatness. Something about their lives gave rise to stories that, whether historical or not, have in them the power to bring truth into our lives.

✛ ✛ ✛

Our pilgrim family begins to break up. Matt and Sarah return to home and jobs. The rest of us make sporadic dashes to other sites—to Ely and St. Etheldreda, to Norwich and Dame Julian. We meet a woman at a church in London who is going in a few days to scatter her father's ashes on Iona, as he had scattered her mother's ashes before.

While in London we have another kind of experience with the holy. We go to the Easter performance of Handel's *Messiah* at Albert Hall. We buy the cheapest seats available, which happen to be directly above and behind the choir, looking over the orchestra and into the conductor's face—the best seats I've ever had for any event. I feel like I'm in the last row of singers.

It is by far the most powerful and moving performance of *Messiah* I have heard, no doubt because Iona and Lindisfarne and Durham have prepared me to hear it more fully. We listen to the play of the vocal parts as they sweep across the massed choir. We hear the individual instruments as each takes its turn in pushing the momentum forward—the musical and narrative momentum of prophecy, birth, life, death, and glorification. During the choral explosion that shouts out Isaiah's catalogue of names for the Messiah—Wonderful Counselor, Almighty God, Everlasting Father, Prince of Peace—the conductor breaks into a smile. I like to think it is because he shares my emotion at the celebration of the attributes of the one I am staking my life and my eternity on, though I know this is unlikely.

During the Hallelujah chorus the entire hall stands, except for the couple sitting next to me. (A different religion? Principled secularists? Nontraditionalists? Simply tired?) Jayne, in contrast, is weeping. For the two of us this is a sacred moment in which art stimulates the emotions of faith. For the couple next to me, and probably for most people in the hall, it is an aesthetic moment, like the sunsets, possibly one connected with a kind of vague nostalgia.

As I sit in Albert Hall, I think back to the previous fall when Jayne and I watched a good friend perform in a play about Handel's *Messiah*. The Celtic Christians have encouraged my conviction that I live in a providential world in which meaningful links extend across time and space. And so I do not think it merely coincidence that we watched Mary in San Diego in November play the role of a lead singer in the first performance of *Messiah*, and that now, on our pilgrimage to the holy, we are seeing Handel's work performed in his adopted city.

Mary played the role of Mrs. Cibber in a play by Tim Slover. At the time that Susannah Cibber sang in the 1742 premier of *Messiah*, first in Dublin, then in London, she was a notorious woman—in an age when notoriety resulted in scorn and social exile rather than, as now, envy and increased success. She was married to Theophilus Cibber, a scoundrel who forced her into the bed of a wealthy degenerate in exchange for money to pay his debts.

A sensational trial ensued. Susannah Cibber was an object of ridicule and contempt. Slover suggests that because she is seen as an unfit parent, her young child has been taken from her. He portrays her, a woman desperate to support and redeem herself, and to recover her child, coming to Handel and asking for a part in his new oratorio.

Handel knows something about scorn and mockery. In the years immediately before *Messiah*, his Italian operas have all been box office failures. The whispers about town say the German pig is washed up. He is contemplating an ignominious return to Germany.

At this low point in his life, Handel writes his greatest work. In twenty-four miraculous days and nights he composes the music for perhaps the most acclaimed work in the western world. A traditional tale, likely as apocryphal as some of the stories about Columba, relates a servant bringing hermit Handel food to his hermitage study and finding him weeping. He says to the servant, "I did think I did see all of heaven open before me, and the great God Himself!"

This is a declaration worthy of a Celtic saint. Handel's music, as surely as any vallum or vision, creates a holy space. The mundane and trivial are pushed back, evil is put on notice. Divine power mingles with divine grace in an announcement about the primacy of the kingdom of God.

Slover, in his play about the first performance of *Messiah,* imagines Handel seeing that he and Susannah Cibber have something in common. Both have been rejected. Both have been scorned. Both know something about grief.

And, in historical fact, it *was* Susannah Cibber who sang the words about Christ in that first *Messiah*: "He was despised and rejected of men. A man of sorrows and acquainted with grief"—words that spoke also of her own life. In the play in San Diego, our friend Mary sang those words, words that applied to Handel as well as to his soloist—words that playwright Slover imagines applying to us all.

There is another story about this first performance of *Messiah*. Susannah Cibber sang those words of sorrow so powerfully that a bishop stood in the audience after her solo and shouted, "Woman, for this, be all thy sins forgiven!" I would like to think this was not a case of the aesthetic trumping the theological, as though artistic excellence yields spiritual merit. I would like to think, rather, that he sensed in her singing a genuine call on God from her own heart, and that God answered that call.

Perhaps I am being sentimental again. I remember once asking the director of a prestigious English boy's choir whether he thought the words of the Bible the boys sang made any impact on them as human beings. The director was puzzled, not about whether it did or not, but about what my question could possibly mean. Bible? Impact? I may as well have asked him how many angels can dance on the head of a choir director.

Perhaps Mrs. Cibber was only singing, not confessing. When I look at the soloists at this Albert Hall performance, I am reminded of how stubbornly earthly we all are. They leave the stage at the end to great applause. From my cheap seat I can see them lining up in the wings to make their curtain call. Just before walking back out on the stage, the woman who has sung the same part as Susannah Cibber adjusts the top of her strapless dress to improve her cleavage. I do not think she is contemplating great spiritual truths.

Whether this performance of *Messiah* has done anyone any good besides Jayne and me, I don't know. The earliest performances certainly did some good. Whenever Handel himself performed the oratorio, he always raised money for charity. His two favorites were orphanages and relief from debtors prisons. The first Dublin performance in 1742 raised enough money to free 142 men imprisoned for poverty. This is an attractive and instructive alignment. A great artistic meditation on even greater spiritual realities results in the physical liberation of many who are, themselves, despised and downtrodden. It is encouraging to think that art and faith—together—can set us free.

✠ ✠ ✠

While in London, Nate and I decide to pay a visit to the *Lindisfarne Gospels* in the British Library. It is my first visit to the British Library since it moved out of its traditional home in the British Museum. The new building on Euston Road has been, inevitably, controversial, panned by some for being an undistinguished pile of red bricks beside the high Victorian pile of red bricks of St. Pancras train station.

My own first impression is more favorable. A pile of red bricks, yes, but a fairly interesting pile—a series of receding horizontals boxes, lots of angles and broken surfaces, the red relieved with green levels and gray roofs. The entrance hall is not disappointing, backed by a six-story glass tower encasing the donated library of King George III. Beautiful books, beautifully housed, and, one hopes, occasionally still read.

On one wall of the entrance hall is a tapestry entitled "If not, not." It is filled with literary allusions, including to Eliot's *The Waste Land*. Nate and I stand before it and pick out as many of the references as we can, as though it is an entry exam in fabric, testing to see who is worthy to pass into the inner sanctum of this shrine to words and ideas. We also discuss our initial reaction to the building and decide it is neither a triumph nor a failure. Few will come just to see the building, but then why should they? As with cathedrals, if people are coming primarily to see the architecture, then the whole enterprise is already in steep decline. All the new library needs to become once again a symbol rather than merely a building is a couple of centuries of people like Marx coming to it and developing ideas that, for better or worse, change the world.

Nate is the most bookish of my kids. I am pleased but not surprised when later in the trip he dashes into a news agent's and comes back with the *International Herald* for news, *USA Today* for sports, and a copy of *The Economist* for light reading. So I know we can stay at the British Library as long as my own legs hold out.

We first take in a temporary exhibition that is sort of like a literary estate sale: everything from Shelley's ashes to Elizabeth Barrett Browning's engagement ring (reminding me that her infamously controlling father had forbidden all of his children to marry). There are children's book exhibits celebrating characters from Pooh to Potter, and recordings of writers like Eliot, Joyce, and Woolf reading their works. Finding a recording of Seamus Heaney reminds me that I had happened to arrive in Ireland the day in 1995 when they announced his winning of the Nobel Prize. I still recall with pleasure the hand-scrawled signs of congratulation and the slightly puffed-out chests of clerks in Irish bookstores. It made me want to be a citizen of a small country, where other people's sorrows and triumphs are felt to be one's own.

As I wander from case to case, breathing in the genius of a thousand years of British literature, I have a small epiphany. I realize I am standing in yet another holy place, the only kind of holiness there is for many. Here we have holy relics—ashes and rings—and holy scriptures—manuscripts handwritten by the literary saints. And, I am forced to confess, these entrance me more than the pieces of Cuthbert's coffin or Columba's stone pillow. I recall St. Jerome's dream. A lover of Roman rhetoric and poetry, he dreams God asks him at the Judgment who he is. When Jerome avers that he is a Christian, God responds, "You are a liar. You are not a Christian but a Ciceronian."

It is not that I love Eliot too much, but that I love God too little. The Celts—pagan and Christian—were enamored of threes, St. Patrick's cloverleaf being only one example. They composed sayings, called triads, one of which reads as follows: "Three sister of lying—perhaps, maybe, guess." I find these three lying-like words often infiltrating my endless interior monologue about the things of faith: perhaps this, maybe that, I guess such and such. I fear I am neither Christian nor Ciceronian—I am Prufrockian. And I worry that the angels will not sing to me.

But we have come here to see a Bible, and so we leave this exhibition and go to the permanent display of the treasures of the empire's library. We take a further step into sacredness, moving from mere genius to the fully inspired. Here are da Vinci's notebooks, Shakespeare's First Folio, the Magna Carta. Unexpectedly, I come across a display of the handwritten score of *Messiah* and study it with ignorant but worshipful eyes, having just been moved by its performance. I take it as a curator's little joke, like the wafer-eating mice in the *Book of Kells*, that near to Handel's score are manuscripts from The Beatles (Lennon's "Imagine" being the pop-secular equivalent of *Messiah*?).

As though Beatles manuscripts aren't wondrous enough, we also find secondary attractions like the Gutenberg Bible, the 1611 King James Bible, various manuscripts of sacred texts from all the world's major religions (what characteristics makes a religion "major"?), and, the one we've come to see, the *Lindisfarne Gospels*. I study closely the two pages open for view and am not disappointed. Nearby is a computer that allows me to see pixilated reproductions of all the pages, requiring me only to drag my finger across the screen to turn the page. Virtual paging through a virtual manuscript–inspiring virtual devotion?

I look especially for the light interlinear script of Aldred, for I know he is a fellow laborer. Aldred was a tenth-century monk at Lindisfarne who wrote on the manuscript a running translation into Anglo-Saxon of the Latin of the gospels. His work would be considered an unforgivable defacement if it were not so important in its own right, the first written translation into the English language of the Bible. I am near the end of a ten-year Bible translation project of my own, and I have often used literal, interlinear translations of the same kind as Aldred's to jump-start my thinking. I imagine him stooped over the precious illuminations of the *Lindisfarne Gospels*, searching the locked closets of his brain, as I often have, for just the right word at just the right place.

✝ ✝ ✝

In early May, Jayne and Anne return home to Minnesota. Now it is only Nate and I. I assume that the pilgrimage part of our adventure is over. I hadn't really planned to spend so much time following around the Celtic saints anyway. It had just worked out that way, and I was glad for it, but now it was time for something different in the ten days we had left.

I figure the Mediterranean – some place we have never been before. I spend hours on the Internet looking for last minute deals to Rhodes or Cyprus or Greece. I finally decide to do what I had heard others do – go to the airport with your bags packed, present yourself at the desk of one of the packaged tour companies and see what presents itself. They hate sending off a charter with empty seats and will sell them for a song on the day of departure.

It works perfectly. One company has a package for a week in Crete, flight included, that is cheaper than staying in the average homeless shelter. I tell them we will take it, and congratulate myself on my cleverness. Unfortunately, after a couple of questions, they decide that they won't take *us*. Turns out Nate's passport will expire in a couple of weeks. No Mediterranean country will allow anyone to enter with less than six weeks left on his or her passport. No exceptions.

All other possibilities are blocked for the same reason. I am disappointed. Our backup plan has been to go to Ireland, but I'm not enthusiastic. I've been to Ireland – three times. Great place, but not a new place. This strikes me as unfair. I almost convince myself I am suffering.

All right then, it will be Ireland. I recall having read in a guidebook about this island off the Ring of Kerry. It's another one of those Celtic places, and so will provide a kind of symmetry to our trip. Of course I wasn't looking for symmetry; I was looking forward to the Mediterranean. But Skellig Michael will have to do.

✠ ✠ ✠

Nate and I get in our rented car at Gatwick and head for southern Wales. Our immediate goal is St. David's, where we will pay our respects to Dewi, The Waterman, as William the Conqueror did in 1081. Dewi was the affectionate shortening of the Welsh name for St. David, the sixth-century patron saint of Wales. The Waterman comes from his abstinence from alcohol, or his purifying of the water at Bath, or his penchant for praying while standing in the cold ocean – or all three. Take your pick.

As we drive into Wales we pass just south of the Wye valley, a place I have visited before in pursuit of Wordsworth. Later I discover that we are near another strange convergence. At this very time, a team of scholar artists in Monmouth, at the top of the Wye valley, is just beginning a new *Book of Kells* – that is, a modern equivalent. And the seeds of the project were sown in my own backyard – in Minnesota.

It is called *The Saint John's Bible*—after its sponsor, Saint John's Abbey and University, which lies, with its Benedictine abbey, just ninety minutes from my Minnesota home. It will be the first handwritten and illustrated Bible since Gutenberg. All the ancient arts of vellum preparation, calligraphy, and illumination are being resurrected to produce an 1,150 page masterpiece two feet tall and, when opened, three feet wide.

I am encouraged that someone cares enough in the twenty-first century to attempt an almost impossibly arduous and complex task for an ultimately spiritual purpose—cares enough to invent a new script, to create 160 illuminations, to gather master craftsmen from various parts of the world. I am glad that they had a ceremony to bless both the chief calligrapher and his tools. I am glad that he reports he was "terrified beyond all reason" as he copied the very first words—at the very time I began this pilgrimage: "This is, after all, the Word of God," he says. I am glad those first words copied were from the opening of the Gospel of John, "In the beginning was the Word, and the Word was God"—words that should both thrill and terrify. I am glad that these illuminations will contain drawings of DNA strands but also Minnesota prairie grass, squirrels, and even, perhaps, a mosquito. Columba may have thought he suffered for God, but he never spent a summer slapping Minnesota mosquitoes. (Or would he have blessed them instead? A true test of sainthood.)

I am glad they are using quill pens, ink sticks, and tempura paints of lapis lazuli (blue), vermilion (red), and malachite (green)—just as they did on Iona and Lindisfarne. I am glad that when the colors have been applied, the artist blows on them softly through a hollow reed. In the biblical languages breath and inspiration and wind all derive from the same word. He is breathing through the reed the inspiration of artistic creation onto the inspired word of God.

I am glad that the calligrapher reports that he can see slight differences in his copying over time that reflect struggles and stress in his private life. And that even though his assistant calligraphers try very hard to use the same script, there are inevitably slight variations in style that will declare always that this was a Bible made entirely by human hands. Perfection of execution is the work of mere machines, Ruskin told the Victorians. We should prize the evidence in any made thing of the tension between human aspiration and human limitation. So should it be in pursuit both of the beautiful and of the holy.

And, oh yes, I am even sanguine about the touch of capitalism in the project. Anyone can buy—shall we say sponsor—a verse for $1,000, or an entire volume for $250,000. I can't quite imagine Columba hitting up local druids to finance his copying, but then again the saints weren't above squeezing donations from surrounding fat cats to carry on the work of the Lord. This too is part of the quotidian quality of spiritual endeavors.

✠ ✠ ✠

Nate and I approach St. David's in late afternoon. A mile or so before town we see a primitive sign at the beginning of a country lane announcing a private room for rent.

We follow the lane down toward the sea and find a small house on the cliffs. A woman and her daughter show us the room and we take it, notwithstanding the sand and grotty bathmat in the tub.

We decide to walk rather than drive into town to see the Cathedral, and are rewarded with a wonderful hike along one of the most beautiful trails in Britain. Looking down from high white cliffs on hidden coves and narrow beaches, we are taking a route that pilgrims have taken for centuries. Eventually we come upon a holy well named after David's mother, and, nearby, the ruins of a chapel on the traditional site of David's birth. The accompanying story indicates that holy men were not always conceived in holiness.

Non, a devout young woman, was raped by the local ruler. She gave birth to David in a field in the middle of a terrible storm, supposedly leaving an imprint of her hand in the stone she clutched during her painful delivery. David performed the usual assortment of miracles, but trumped the other saints by starting before he was born. The story goes that Non, when pregnant, entered a church while St. Gildas was preaching. He was immediately struck dumb and was unable to finish his sermon, an indication that the *in utero* little saint-in-the-making was destined to be a great speaker.

Nate and I eventually get to St. David's Cathedral, built long after the saint's wooden monastery had disappeared. The Cathedral is in a valley, only its spire visible from any distance, apparently an attempt to keep out of sight of coastal pirates active at the time it was built. The setting makes it look smaller than it is, but also increases the sense of intimacy. It looks approachable, a place where even sinners might hope to be received. We are in time for evensong.

Church services in British cathedrals often strike me as a little sad. To begin with, almost no one shows up. Nate and I double the attendance at this one. The archetypal mid-week Anglican service, in my experience, comprises a priest, two old women, one old man, a couple of others in their forties or fifties, and, if things are booming, a smattering of tourists. The locals help the priest get through the liturgy while the tourists rubber-neck the roof and stained glass and hope they haven't committed themselves to anything that lasts more than twenty minutes.

Beyond the shortage of bodies, there is the inescapable sense that the glory days are long gone. These grand buildings were created by people–by entire communities–that believed without question in the stories told in their windows. The churches were expressions in stone and glass of the prior commitments of their hearts and minds. They were, in that sense, as natural as the blossoming of an apple tree. They grew with logical inevitability from the hands of men and women with a certain understanding of the world. That understanding has been in decline in Britain for decades, perhaps centuries. It now competes with football, shopping, and tending the garden, and does not fare well with the masses.

I do not think Dewi would have cared. It is said that if you wanted to join his monastery you were made to wait outside for ten days, during which time you were refused entry, spoken to harshly, and given painful tasks to do. If you were still around at the end, they would give some thought to your candidacy. No church growth fan, Dewi. We Americans, in contrast, turn our sanctuaries into lounges, our worship services into variety shows, and our theology into sugary mush in hopes that someone will like us. Maybe we could learn something from Dewi—give me a few good men and women, slackers be damned.

After evensong we take a quick look around the church. We discover a box in the wall that traditionally has been thought to hold Dewi's bones. Killjoy scientists have recently declared it is not so. I recall Ruskin's melancholy lament when the new science of geology was wreaking havoc on naïve versions of nineteenth-century religious faith: "If only the Geologists would let me alone, I could do very well, but those dreadful hammers! I hear the clink of them at the end of every cadence of the Bible verses."

If Dewi's bones cannot be of much help to us, perhaps his last words to his disciples can be. "Perform the small things," he told them, "as you have seen me do." Here, it may be, is the essence of the holy life: bringing holiness into this world small act by small act. Why, Christ asked his disciples, do you call me Lord and yet not do the things I tell you? It is a question without wiggle room. The people I have encountered on this pilgrimage matched, to the best of their abilities, their faith and values with their actions, and thereby won the affection of the common folk and became, along the way, saints—a designation given them by the people, not, to this day, by the official church.

✠ ✠ ✠

From St. David's we hovercraft to Ireland. What would Columba and the others have thought of the equivalent of a small town–complete with casino, restaurants, and movie theater–flying across the waves on air? A miracle? An abomination?

We head toward Dublin but check off two holy spots along the way. We are veteran pilgrims now. It takes a lot to impress us. St. Brigid's holy well in Kildare fails to do so. A bit of stone, a bit of water, and little bits of cloth tied in the surrounding bushes to symbolize a worry left behind. We've been there and done that when it comes to holy wells.

I am more impressed by how one–or is it two–traffic lights in the small town of Kildare can back up cars for miles in both directions on this major road between Dublin and the south. I am tempted to say that all this traffic is an affront to the memory of Brigid, but consider the following from Cogitosus, her hagiographer: "Who can count the different crowds and numberless peoples flocking in from all the provinces–some for the abundant feasting, others for the healing of their afflictions, others to watch the pageant of the crowds, others with great gifts and offerings." It is a reminder that monasteries in those days, far from being isolated outposts, were most often founded near existing settlements and became centers of civilizing activity.

Brigid is one of the big three of Irish saints–along with Patrick and Columba–but Nate and I can allot her only thirty minutes. It seems miserly of us for a saint whose defining characteristic was generosity. Brigid apparently had this irrepressible urge to give things away to the poor–

including her mother's butter and her father's prized sword. She is a big attraction to current Celticphiles because she represents a strong woman in a position of leadership in the supposedly more egalitarian Celtic church. She founded one of the few double monasteries—one for women and one for men. Clearly she deserves more time—and more reflection—but Nate and I want to be in Dublin by dark and we still have to squeeze in St. Kevin.

We pass the time in the car on the way to Glendalough listening to Irish radio and get a short but sharp lesson in the Irish gifts for excitability and feeling persecuted. The host of the show is interviewing his guest about the great crisis that has arisen in our time because of the high costs of a liquor license in Ireland. The guest is making the case as best he can but not, apparently, with enough emotion. The host gets more and more exercised about the issue, a modern Potato Famine, and soon is doing all the talking.

"It's a crying shame, it is. It cost hundreds of thousands of punts for a license and the corporations are bent on keeping it that way. Why a young man can't even hope to get a start in the drinks business today!"

His guest is reduced to supporting from the sidelines. "That's right."

"There's a dearth of pubs today in Dublin, an absolute dearth!" the host continues.

Nate and I laugh, trying our best to mimic high Irish dudgeon. "A dearth of pubs in Dublin!" we say together. It is not a dearth that any non-Irishman is likely to notice, finding at least as many pubs as street lights in the typical Irish town, but it is fitting that we hear this sad tale as we are leaving Brigid's territory. She might well have sympathized with the man on the radio, given that one of her most popular miracle stories has her bath water turning into beer. And in a tenth-century poem, St. Brigid wishes the blessing of good drink on Christ himself:

> *I should like a great lake of ale*
> *For the King of kings;*
> *I should like the family of Heaven*
> *To be drinking it through time eternal.*

✠ ✠ ✠

Glendalough is in the Wicklow Mountains south of Dublin. We drive over the pass from Kildare and into the wooded vale with the two small lakes that was Kevin's home so many centuries ago. It is 5:30 in the afternoon and we catch the last showing of the documentary at the visitor center just before it closes. As usual we find that Kevin is a saint about whom much is said but little is known. One story reports he stood so long and so still at prayer with arms outstretched that a bird built a nest in his hand, obliging him to continue standing there until the baby birds had hatched and flown away.

Glendalough is deceptively beautiful. The natural beauty is transparent–steep, wooded hills protecting two small, idyllic lakes; a broad walking path through trees and meadows and ferns. The deceptive part is my feeling that holiness might be easier in a place this edenic. Even I could be devout, I'm tempted to think, in a place so obviously fashioned to evoke peace and worship.

I think this way because I come here two hundred years

after the English Romantic poets, who taught us to seek out natural beauty and to look there for the Power behind it (as with us moderns, they often tried to avoid the G word). In contrast, this valley most likely seemed a frightening and off-putting place when Kevin first came, living for seven years in utter solitude. Medieval people tended to see the woods as the haunts of demons and vicious animals. They were a place where it was easy to die. You did not go there to relax and recharge your batteries.

In fact, the area around Upper Lake where Kevin first lived is called St. Kevin's Desert. The forest *was* a desert—a place of desolation and abandonment—to the hermits who first sought them ought. Any place away from the scattered clusters of human beings—there were no cities in Ireland before the Vikings—was, literally, a desert(ed) place.

Glendalough did not stay a desert for long. Word of Kevin's holiness began to spread, and others arrived to be near the holy man. He resisted at first, but then accepted his responsibility to create a community for those wishing to so shape their lives as to draw down God amongst them.

As on Iona and Lindisfarne, and as at most every other monastery of the time, they built encircling walls to mark off a holy space. Over the years, and then the centuries, many buildings arose, first of wood and then of stone; in the tenth or eleventh century an impressive round tower stuck its head above the trees. Eventually Glendalough became one of the largest monasteries in Ireland, enough so to earn the name "monastic city."

The roofless ruins of the main church invite our inspection. Here the monks came every few hours throughout the day to worship and pray. Kevin, poet-saint, wrote a Rule for them in verse. Every night two monks stayed behind to recite Psalms until morning. I think it would be comforting to live in a community where someone is reciting sacred poetry as I sleep.

The remains of this monastic city are still very impressive. No one walks through them without taking a picture of the hundred-foot tower, us included. Most stop to contemplate St. Kevin's grand high cross. But the thing that most moves me about the monastic enclosure is a small detail.

At the entrance to the monastic site are double arches a few strides apart—most likely once supporting a stone roof. And just inside the entrance, on the right-hand side as you walk in, is a large stone slab in the wall with a simple, almost crudely simple, cross etched into it. The cross, undoubtedly, marks the point at which the holy space begins. It was the point where a refugee or even criminal would know that he or she was safe, at least for a while. And there were many things to seek refuge from in medieval Ireland.

I am attracted to the possibility that there are places of refuge in the world—physical places, spiritual places. To one degree or another we are all refuge seekers. The trick is to find a true refuge and not an illusory one, and I feel that there is true refuge somewhere here about.

And I like that today, at this moment, there is a bicycle leaning against the cross, placed there without thought by someone looking around. Antiquarians and preservations would be horrified. The handle bar and pedal might easily scratch the stone within the cross. But the bike is not the first thing that has leaned against this cross, and the mix of the holy and the everyday seems right.

Nate and I do not have time to dwell in this monastic city. Evening is coming on and we have miles to go before we sleep. We leave the ruins and walk along the trail that leads toward the back of the valley. The deepening shadows of the large trees and steep hillside hang over the path. No one is around and we can hear the still, small voice passing through the branches that whispered to Kevin (as to Elijah before him). One of us observes that this moment feels a lot like Tolkien, and we like two members of the Fellowship on a ring quest.

After a meditative twenty-minute walk we see a sign directing us up the hillside to St. Kevin's Cell. We make the short, steep climb and find ourselves at a small circle of stones on a little promontory with the lake visible below between the trees. We sit quietly, apart, and do not speak.

As elsewhere, I give my imagination the task of turning me into the saint and making this my cell and these my woods and my job that of finding God. And as usual, my imagination is not quite up to the assignment. The guidebook quotes the Egyptian desert fathers: "Go sit in your cell and your cell will teach you everything." I know this command has wisdom in it, but I also know I will not wait here long enough to find what Kevin's cell has to teach.

✠ ✠ ✠

Before nightfall Nate and I are on the way to Dublin. I expect it will be easy to find an affordable and inhabitable B&B in the suburbs. I am wrong. The places we scare up with the help of our guidebook are either too dumpy or too expensive or both. We even try a Catholic retreat house, knowing they sometimes have simple rooms, but no one answers the door. So much for the ancient tradition of monastic hospitality. Eventually we find, unlike Christ, a place to lay our heads.

Our primary goal the next day is to see the *Book of Kells* at Trinity College. I had seen it first in 1983, but it made little impression on me—a famous old book in a famous old library, opened arbitrarily to reveal two pages of illuminated text. This time I go carefully through the fine exhibit since installed and look at everything with wonder. Greater knowledge and experience have bred greater reverence.

My differing responses to the same stimulus suggest another truth: Those unprepared for the sacred are unlikely to experience it. Similarly, any experience of the holy enlarges one's capacity to experience it again. In 1983 the *Book of Kells* was simply something else I knew I was supposed to see while in Dublin. Now it is as much a personal icon as anything can be an icon for a boy raised Baptist on the plains of Texas during the Eisenhower years. Because now I had been to Iona. I had sat on the grassy slopes overlooking the sound where it first came into being. I knew better the conditions under which it was crafted. I knew better the devotion to knowledge and art and the imagination and God that had led these monks to pour love into their labor. I could look now at those filigreed testaments of faithfulness and hope for some of those same qualities in my own life.

The details in the fully illuminated pages are so pro-fuse, so small, and so interconnected that I feel I cannot see what I am seeing. Lion head biting red fish, itself being bitten by black fish–or are they fish?–their impossibly long and sinuous bodies intertwined like a child's maze, all three creatures, and at least three others, contained in an intricate border of further filigree–this entire mini-world no larger than the face of a watch, all trapped within the coiled tail of the letter T beginning the first word of the page of folio 124R. I need it all magnified and explained.

I get the same feeling when trying to step back and assess my own life–pattern within pattern, detail in sup-port of (and yet lost within) the whole, seeming randomness morphing into providential intersection–and yet I can see it all only as in a glass darkly. And I sometimes wonder if the pattern is there at all. What Giraldus said of the drawings in the *Book of Kells* in the twelfth century seems equally true of the events of my life here in the twenty-first: "If you look at them carelessly and casually and not too closely, you may judge them to be mere daubs rather than careful compositions. You will see nothing subtle where everything is subtle."

Images of Christ abound. Often he looks something like a 1960s California surfer–young, yellow-haired, and sport-ing an attitude. When not depicted quasi-naturalistically, he is present in a wide array of symbols: fish, lion, snake, and peacock. If the snake throws you–isn't Satan supposed to be the serpent?–you aren't thinking like a Celt. Think shedding of skin as a symbol of resurrection. Actually an allusion to Satan is included too–that is, an allusion to the

snake's seduction of Eve, the subsequent Fall, and, therefore, the need for this yellow-headed Savior.

There are enough animals hidden away in the *Book of
Kells* to fill the Ark, and they aren't there just to relieve the
tedium of the occasional genealogy. Not only are they often
symbolic in themselves, they frequently come at a point
that reinforces the text. Peacocks, for instance, are a symbol of incorruptibility. On a page describing the women
approaching Christ's tomb, thinking wrongly that they are
going to prepare a body against decay, the letter *U* in the
word *Una* is filled with two peacocks. For those with eyes
to see, and a Celtic understanding of symbols, this tiny
bit of art prepares us for the wonderful reality that the
women – and we – are about to experience.

The exhibit at Trinity also includes information on
other early Irish illuminated Bibles. I am struck by one
of them that depicts a gospel writer holding the Bible
not directly in this hand, but with his hand covered by
his robe. I have no idea what symbolism is meant, but I
immediately think "too hot to handle" – that is, too holy to
handle. "This book," it says to me, "is dangerous stuff. It
could explode in your face. Handle with care!" A lifetime
of asbestos sermons, insipid preachments, and selective cul-
ture-conforming applications has obscured this fact for me.
I am glad for the reminder.

If I think of these illuminated Bibles as time bombs in
beautiful packaging, others think only of the packaging.
At what point I wonder, did the *Book of Kells* change from
being first of all the word of God to being first of all a mar-
velous example of early medieval art? When did its value

shift from what it said to how it was presented? The ones who made it could keep these two things together. Fewer and fewer can do so today.

chapter five

To Skellig Michael – Monastery in the Sky

Who could show me a solitude, a place without roads?
      Evagrius of Antioch

It is possible to be a solitary in one's mind while living in a crowd,
and it is possible for one who is a solitary
to live in the crowd of his own thoughts.
      Amma Syncletica

And, finally, there is Skellig Michael. I claimed at the beginning it couldn't be described, but the Celtic saints have taught me the fascination of the impossible.

I expect the usual visitor center and gift shop. Instead, the voice of the fisherman's wife on the phone says, "Be at the Portmagee pier at 10:30 tomorrow morning. If the weather is good enough, my husband will be there in his boat to pick you up." The weather the next day is unusually fine, and down the inlet we watch him chug, Nate and I, his only passengers for the day.

We hop on board and start out toward the sea. The engine of the fishing boat is loud enough to make talking difficult and it fills the air with diesel fumes. Still, we are far better off than earlier pilgrims, who have been coming to the island for a thousand years. In the nineteenth century the eight-mile trip to Skellig required hiring a rowboat and four oarsmen. By 1960 tourist trips to the island were fairly rare. But an apparent increase in spiritual hunger in recent decades has created, as in the distant past, a steady stream of people showing up to be ferried to one of earth's thin places.

It's just under an hour out to Skellig Michael, depending on your boat and the conditions. You don't see the island when you start out from the harbor, but soon you are passing looming Bray's Head and there it is on the horizon, the first step into the Atlantic. Tiny at first, it's shrouded today in a thin white haze. It looks mystical – in part because I expect it to look mystical. I think of Avalon, the island to which King Arthur was carried on the barge of singing women, there to recover from his wounds and, someday, return again to a new Camelot. Will my own wounds be soothed today?

And as I think of Avalon, I wonder why I must always explain these experiences to myself in terms of poems and writers and other places. Perhaps, like most people, I can't stand the holy at full strength. I need it mediated – through a poem, through a biography, through a story – through an island. I go to Iona and Lindisfarne and Skellig Michael to get a tangible taste of an intangible and fearful reality. But I want only a taste. Like the Israelites at Sinai, I want God to speak to Moses, not to me.

Approaching Skellig Michael from the north, we are

following a path taken so many centuries ago by a boat-load of monks looking for a place to battle the flesh and the devil. They saw themselves as engaged in a war whose object was to be like Christ—that is, to be more like what they were created to be. They saw themselves as spiritual warriors. Their aim, however, was not to kill someone else, but to destroy false selves, to shed counterfeit versions of their own life, so that they might help bring into reality the kingdom of the High King of Heaven.

The man in charge of the search is traditionally reported to be St. Finnian. But which Finnian? Was it Finnian of Clonard? That Finnian studied in Wales under David and then returned to found Clonard, a monastery that became widely known for learning and a place where both Columba and Brendan the Navigator were pupils. Or was it Finnian of Moville, Columba's mentor from whom he "stole" the copy of the book that may have launched a war and a journey to Iona?

In fact, neither man's dates fit well with the supposed late sixth-century founding of Skellig Michael. There are other Finnians, but the truth is we don't know who founded the Skellig monastery or exactly when. If who and when are uncertain, most puzzling of all, when I finally see the place, is why.

As is so often the case in fable and tale, we have a harbinger that we are approaching a special place. About half way out, I spot a dart of color winging past the boat at frantic speed. It is a puffin, that compact burst of bird and bill that spends the majority of its life in air and water, touching the land only in obscure places to devote a short time to the birth, feeding, and protection of a puffin chick.

Puffins come to Skellig Michael at the same time we had come to England, in late March, their bills in the process of changing color from the dull yellow of winter to bright red, blue, and yellow of summer. It is May now and they have taken over Skellig rabbit holes and other burrows. But they have approached Skellig Michael cautiously, as I am doing. When the puffins first arrive from unmarked journeys in the North Atlantic, they keep their distance from the island, floating for days in the sea, within sight, but not venturing on the island itself.

I understand their caution. If Skellig Michael is, as they say, a sacred place, then I'm not sure I want to be there. I remember what happened to the poor sap who tried to steady the Ark of the Covenant when it was falling off the wagon. Iona and Lindisfarne have small numbers of people living safely on them today, undoubtedly a few no better than I am. But Skellig Michael is now alone again, severe and solitary, not a place you'd want to spend the night. Perhaps it does not suffer tourists gladly.

But I will take heart from the puffins. After days of eyeing Skellig Michael from afar, a handful of them will land on the island at dusk and spend the night. That serves as a signal to the rest, and in a matter of forty-eight hours in mid-April the entire flock will swarm ashore. If there is a puffin avant-garde on Skellig Michael, there has, through the ages, also been an unbroken ribbon of spiritual seekers who have come here, for an hour or for a lifetime, to test its possibilities for spiritual discovery. I will follow their lead.

Actually there are two islands. Little Skellig, a short

distance away, is a bird sanctuary, home not only to puffins but to razorbills, guillemots, kittiwakes, petrels, and, most evident of all, more than 20,000 nesting pairs of gannets. From a distance I discern a kind of confusion in the air over the island. As we come closer, I see it is a furious canopy of flying birds.

Our captain brings the boat to within a few feet of Little Skellig, taking us expertly through narrow passages and into tiny coves for a better view of the nests and the seals. Little Skellig is a small city of winged citizens, lining by the thousands every ledge and landing, announcing to the universe in their distinctive squawks their rights of position and place. I've seen the same among my own kind.

A bird lover would be more than content with Little Skellig. But a human watcher soon casts his eyes over to Skellig Michael, a mile and a half away. I can understand why birds would choose this place, miles out to sea, but why men?

Skellig Michael, like two other famous monastic islands I have visited in years past, is named for the archangel, who reputedly came to Ireland to help Patrick with the snakes and the demons. But that name came later. When that first boat load of monks approached, it was only a *skeilic*—a stone island—one of many islands off the west coast of Ireland. Why did they choose this one? What seemed promising? What made them hopeful? What told them that God was better to be found or served here than at the place they came from?

Perhaps they liked that it points to the sky. Skellig Michael is 714 feet of stony verticality, a natural Gothic cathedral with narrow spikes of eroded rock decorating it like gargoyles. It has twin peaks, one at each end, like the fingertips of two parted hands lifted to heaven. Making no compromise with horizontal reality, it thrusts straight up from the sea floor to the clouds. Any living thing that dares to ride its audacious breaching of the sea will have to hold on for dear life.

Fittingly, there is no place for our boat to tie up. Skellig Michael is little more accessible now than it was 1,400 years ago when the monks arrived. Nate and I jump off the boat onto a concrete platform that has been stuck like a limpet to the base of a cliff—on an island that is all cliffs. The captain backs the boat away, telling us he will wait out in the ocean until he sees we have returned to the platform. I find myself hoping he is a vigilant and reliable man.

My first response to actually stepping foot on Skellig Michael is disappointment. I know very little about the island, but had read in a guidebook about the romantically precarious steps up the steep sides that had been carved or placed by the original medieval monastic community. Instead I find myself walking up a wide, gently sloping concrete path. Is this somebody's bright idea for making the island more manageable for effete modern pilgrims?

Thankfully it is not. I am walking what is generously called the lighthouse road. In 1820 construction began on two lighthouses on Skellig Michael to alleviate the ancient scourge of shipwreck in this part of Ireland, where hungry rock and thin-skinned ship have been coming disastrously together since human beings first pushed off from shore.

The builders of the lighthouse road, as builders are

wont, cared little for what had been there before them. In blowing away enough rock to allow this slender thread of concrete to wind along the southern base of Skellig Michael, they also blew away the lower approach of the monks' stone ladder to the top of the island. So now we must walk a few minutes on a narrow nineteenth-century concrete road in order to reach the medieval steps that will take us higher.

Actually there are three ancient pathways to the top of Skellig Michael. An eastern ascent begins near the landing platform and another path starts out from Blue Cove on the northern side of the island. Today there are only a handful of days a year during which a boat could successfully approach the northern steps, part of the evidence that climatic conditions were different in the first few centuries of monastic life than they are today.

Three paths up the mountain. It reminds me of the favorite metaphor of religious universalists. "There are many paths up the mountain," they say, suggesting that most all quests for the spiritual are equally valid. It is a tempting view, one that certainly fits nicely with our modern let's get along, affirm everybody, who-are-you-to-say mood.

But the metaphor takes a mysterious turn on Skellig Michael. In addition to the southern ascent, there are also on the south side fourteen steps carved into solid stone that begin in the middle of nowhere in particular and lead further on to more nowhere. They do not start at the sea nor do they end in the heights. They are simply there, testimony to an unfulfilled idea—begun in hope, buttressed with sweat, but left hanging, in process and in stone.

No, I do not believe that all paths lead to the top of the mountain. Some lead off cliffs. Some rise promisingly for a ways but then descend back to the base. And some, like the fourteen Skellig steps, lead nowhere at all.

Where, I wonder, is my own path leading?

✚ ✚ ✚

The lighthouse road intersects in a few hundred yards with the southern ascent. I am glad for it. Here, finally, is the real thing, the authentic stuff, the guidebook-promised tangible evidence of ancient spirituality. I am thankful for the steps – until I start to climb them.

I let Nate go first. No use standing in the way of eager youth. The first fifty are a delight. I study each one, trying to picture the monk who dug with maddox into the side of the cliff and the no less than two monks who would have been necessary to wrestle the thick stone slab into place.

The next fifty are also no problem for this now travel-hardened pilgrim. If after still fifty more steps I am now breathing a bit heavily, what of it? Pilgrimage is supposed to include discomfort; besides, the view is growing more spectacular with every step.

And so fifty more steps, and then another fifty.

Have you ever noticed how irrelevant spectacular scenery is to a hiker in pain? How the scope of the world narrows to the tips of your shoes and the few feet of ground immediately in front of you? It is the same with spiritual climbing. The books and brochures promise mountaintop vistas, closeness to God, serenity and peace; they don't mention that getting there, if one ever does, is a lot like a death march.

But what are another fifty steps among pilgrims? Nate is patient with me, stopping whenever he sees me staring too closely at the steep steps just a few inches from my bowed and bobbing head. So that makes, what, three hundred steps?

It is good that I don't know at this point what I will learn later. There are some 2,300 steps on Skellig Michael, not counting the lighthouse road. I have only climbed a bit over ten percent of them and already I have forgotten why I came. I have forgotten everything I have read and seen in the last six weeks. I do not recall Columba or Aidan or Cuthbert or hills where angels came down. I know only that my thighs are burning and I am again in danger of feeling sorry for myself.

Does the spiritual have a snowball's chance in hell as long as we are tethered to these bodies? I know I shouldn't use a word like *tethered*. I know I am supposed to celebrate the God-created physicality of things – that's what all the balanced people tell me, the Celtic saints included. But the body *is* a nuisance sometimes. It is so needy and whiney and insistent on getting what it wants. It is the perennial two-year-old child of our existence. And so I sit for a while and rest.

The rest does me good. The sun is warm and the breeze cool – these are physical too. I feel lucky to be here, a place I hadn't even heard of a year before. I feel lucky to be here with Nate, my anamchara for this journey. And I am luckier than I know. There may indeed be 2,300 steps on Skellig Michael, but only 600 are on this southern ascent. I am halfway there – though at this point I don't know where *there* is.

Another few hundred steps takes us to Christ's Saddle, the only open patch of ground on the island, and the place I assume I am climbing to. Christ's Saddle, so named by the monks, is a small scrap of ground (less than half an acre it appears to me, though I am no good at estimating such things) that lies between the two peaks of Skellig Michael, which tower over it on either side.

It would be too generous to call it level; there is no such thing on the island. It is more of a hump – a saddle. Walk a few dozen yards across to the north side and you find yourself staring down at birds flying beneath you, the sea acting as a green backdrop 500 feet below. It's disorienting to be looking down at flying birds, and I back away from the deadly attraction-repulsion of great heights.

Nate and I walk toward South Peak, climbing a few yards up its base until the grass runs out and further climbing seems impossible. We sit in the warm sun and look at the small place where I imagine the monks working this bit of soil, which some think was brought here from the mainland, basket by basket, by the monks themselves. After this tiring ascent I have both great admiration for the successive groups of twelve or so men who lived here for 600 years – and great questions about their sanity.

After visiting in 1910, George Bernard Shaw called Skellig Michael "an incredible, impossible, mad place. I tell you the thing does not belong to any world that you and I have lived and worked in; it is part of our dream world." I understand what Shaw is saying, but the sweat running down my back is not a dream. And it was real sweat for those monks who scampered up and down the cliffs, snatching eggs from bird nests on rocky ledges high above the sea. And it was real sweat when they were killing seals for meat and skins to trade with passing sailors for fishing hooks and staples, and when they were growing small patches of grain in this little bit of soil hundreds of feet in the air between the two peaks of the island. It is important to remember the reality of that sweat, because we must keep these men like us if they are to do us any good.

I am also feeling real hunger at the moment. Nate had refused breakfast this morning because he had decided to fast for the day. I was unprepared for it but not surprised. My kids often do in practice the things I heartily support in theory. Given Nate's plan to fast, my uneaten bowl of cereal before me had seemed suddenly gluttonous. I announced I would be happy to join him, and now my stomach was asking whether I hadn't been a bit impulsive.

I look out over the sea and spot our boat, waiting patiently, as promised, for us to have our pilgrim experience. The sight of it is comforting, assuring me of the needed escape when I've had enough of the sacred.

It is not hard, however, to picture another time and another boat whose sighting would have brought a gasp and a sick feeling in the stomach—a Viking boat. Viking raiders first struck an Irish monastery in 795, two years after their initial Lindisfarne attack. It was just a matter of time before they found the little community of monks sitting atop this isolated rock off the coast of Kerry.

The Irish called them Finngaill—the fair foreigners. They were the stateless terrorists of their day, which is exactly how John Henry Newman described them: "They ravaged far and wide at will, and no retaliation on them was possible, for these pirates … had not a yard of territory, a town, or a fort, no property but their vessels, no subjects but their crews."

They traveled on the superhighways of the time—the open seas. Their dragon-headed longboats could be up to 130 feet in length and carry hundreds of men, and could land almost anywhere. More often they were smaller, with a typical crew of thirty to forty, but these smaller craft could attack in fleets of dozens.

Or alone. It would not have taken a fleet to pillage Skellig Michael. One ship could appear on the horizon. It would not have had to be in a hurry. Where were the monks to go? Iona, though small, is filled with rocky hills and crags that could provide some protection. Lindisfarne, though open and flat, is very near the mainland, to which the monks could flee. But Skellig Michael is the equivalent of a modern-day office tower. If death is approaching from below, there is nothing to do but wait or jump.

The Skellig Michael monastery, unlike others, was not a rich morsel for the Vikings. Barely a crumb. It would have had a minimum of the liturgical instruments made of precious metals, and sometimes jewels, that the Vikings were looking for. But it was a place to pillage, and pillaging was their call.

The first recorded Viking attack on Skellig Michael took place in 812. They had a habit of coming back, checking in every few years on places they had raided before to see what restocking might have gone on. They paid another visit to Skellig Michael in 823 and this time took the abbot with them. The *Annals of Innisfallen* does not tell us much, but enough to give an insight into Viking cruelty: "Scelec was plundered by the heathens and Itgal was carried off into captivity, and he died of hunger on their hands." A man hardened by a lifetime of fasting does not starve quickly. But the Vikings apparently were in no hurry.

The *Annals* calls them "heathens." That is not an acceptable word today. We are told it is intolerant to use any word that suggests that one way up the mountain is superior to another. One man's heathenism is another man's indigenous religion. But as I sit now next to South Peak on Christ's Saddle, imagining a Viking boat sailing patiently but inexorably toward me, laughter and taunts coming over the water, mixing with the cry of birds, I am not inclined to imagine that I am seeing the approach of fellow spiritual seekers.

The Vikings came again in 833 and 839. It must have changed the way the monks of Skellig Michael perceived their place in the world. They had come there in imitation of the Desert Fathers of the fourth century, whom Irish Christians greatly admired. Early Christians went to the deserts of Egypt and elsewhere for many reasons, but primarily to escape everything that would distract them from their dance with God.

Most of those distractions were embodied in civilization—in cities and empires, in getting and spending, in making and selling, in marrying and child-rearing, in all the endless activities and contacts entailed in living with others. All these horizontal demands were seen as the enemy of the main purpose of our creation—to know and be in right relationship with the God who made us. The desert was attractive to these earliest of Christians, as Thomas Merton has pointed out, precisely because there was nothing there. It was an empty space—empty of people, governments, markets, and trivial demands—waiting to be filled with spiritual significance.

We are quite sure today that these people were, to be polite, misguided—possibly disturbed. Some sat for years on tall pillars, some starved themselves into vision-filled stupors, some competed with each other to win triathlons of the soul.

We think they were deluded, but the Irish thought they were grand. They lamented that they had no deserts of their own to retreat to, so they settled for the wooded deserts of the forests, and the stony deserts of the anchorage, and the blue-green deserts of the sea.

When the first monks saw Skellig Michael, they saw a desert—a place away. Sitting in their cells at 600 feet they were higher and more isolated even than Simon Stylites on his sixty-foot pillar. They were free to do what was important in life.

For two hundred years that dearly loved isolation must have seemed almost complete. They surely had some regular contact with the mainland for they would have needed to be supplied bread for communion. And they had the occasional visitor or new member. But contact with the rest of the world was infrequent and at their own choosing.

The Viking raids changed all that. The Irish desert had been violated, and could be again at any time. The monks likely did not fear death from the fair foreigners.

They feared violation of their sacred space and their sacred routine. It was no longer possible to leave the world. The world had come to them–bearing swords.

I say they did not fear death from the Vikings, but of course that is true only in the abstract. A monk, watching from Christ's Saddle as a group of axe-wielding, blood-seeking Vikings climbed up the very steps Nate and I had climbed, could not have helped but be afraid. No amount of piety and prioritized thinking can keep the heart from racing in the face of someone wanting to put a hatchet in your forehead.

But at the same time that their adrenaline was surging, they were likely to be more concerned that they die well. As Geoffrey Moorhouse has put it, "If they were to die, they hoped to do so fully recognised for what they were." He imagines them gathering to say the Lord's Prayer after they first see the Viking ship, and then scattering to hide what few holy objects they possess among the rocks.

I am both intrigued and convicted by the phrase "fully recognised for what they were." We live in a culture in which serious religious faith is slightly embarrassing. Faith is seen as possibly a value–something hoped for–and not as a fact–something known. It is benign or even useful for food drives and homeless shelters, but ugly and even dangerous when it publicly asserts its claims as truth. Therefore it is asked to stay private, to speak only when spoken to, to stay in the corner and mind its very limited business.

The Celtic Christians could not have imagined such a thing. All of life was to be organized in light of spiritual realities. There was not a separate truth for monks and for kings, and when kings needed correcting, they were corrected. In the meantime, daily life was an ordered rhythm of worship, work, and study–all as an offering to God. That at least was the intent, though of course human nature often exacted its due.

I am more a modern man than a Celtic Christian in this regard. I want to be polite. I want to get along. When alone in a restaurant, I do not bow my head over meals. I do not cite the Bible in making arguments to people who put little value in it. I do not want anyone organizing prayer in public schools. I do not want my political leaders invoking God as the source of their every policy. And, in the same spirit, I try not to roll my eyes when my colleagues start talking about going to psychics or of prosperity energy fields in their homes.

But I wonder if I am so eager to fit in that I am afraid to be "fully recognised" for what I am. Would I have knelt in prayer as that out of breath Viking raised his axe over me on Christ's Saddle, or might I have offered to show him where the treasures were hidden in hopes of continued life? More to the point, how willing am I to organize my own life and actions and relationships around those spiritual truths that I claim should define every life? How eager am I to be fully recognized?

If these monks and holy men and women did not much fear death, they did fear judgment–especially *the* Judgment. When Brendan the Navigator, born only a short distance from Skellig Michael, was dying, he was asked what he feared. His honest answer reveals his greatest fears were not for the moment of death itself, but for what came after: "I fear going alone, for the journey is dark. I fear the unknown, the presence of the King, the sentence of the Judge."

Brendan feared being in God's presence because he believed God was fearfully awesome and that Moses was allowed for his own safety to see only God's back through a crack in the rock. He feared God's judgment because he believed that ultimate holiness was incompatible with sin and he knew himself to be a willful sinner. Only the grace of God could save him from a deserved and terrible eternal fate.

We are sure, today, that we know better. You can't scare us with your pointy-tailed devils and everlasting fires. Hieronymous Bosch paintings are examples of an artistic style not of an eternal fate. If there is a God at all, he is all love, love, love. No unpleasantness, everybody makes it. I'm okay, you're okay, and God's okay with both of us.

Never mind that this would not be love but indifference, not love but merely looking the other way. As if God is saying, "Didn't really mean it. Just Ten Suggestions. No offense taken. Come on in." I do not have a clear or legalistic picture of the afterlife. I do not envision pitchforks or divinely-sanctioned torture. But I do believe Brendan was right to be deeply concerned about meeting a King and a Judge.

✛ ✛ ✛

Scholars protest the popular image of the Vikings—a generic term for a variety of northern European groups—as horned, heathen, marauding savages (no horns, in reality, and plenty of civilization). The Irish experience bears this out. Not only did the raiders eventually decide to stay – establishing the towns of Dublin, Cork, Waterford, and Limerick, among others – they eventually embraced the Christian faith of their favorite targets. The descendents of those who starved Abbot Itgal were worshipping his God not too long after.

This makes me wonder about the ebb and flow between paganism and faith over the millennia. The historical face of my own faith appeared in present-day Iraq something like 4,000 years ago. It took a defining turn 2,000 years later. Through all those first 2,000 years it was a tiny minority enterprise in the midst of great empires. Then it got much smaller.

Pushed out of the Jewish culture that nurtured it, it left Palestine for Africa and Europe just before the Romans crushed Israel in A.D. 70. Finding a home among the poor and outcast, it was spread by persecution and rejection throughout an empire that first tried to kill it and then bestowed on it the mixed blessing of official approval. It rode the Roman coattails into northern Europe, as far as places on the edge of the world like Ireland.

My path up the mountain was in the ascendancy, at least in this large part of the world. Paganism was in retreat. The one, true God was becoming known. Darkness, I like to think, was retreating before the light.

But then Rome, like all earthly kingdoms, unraveled. Christianity retreated from Europe. Old ways and old understandings returned. And so it stayed for centuries, until small lights began to glow from the edge, from the extremes, from the likes of Ireland, and slowly, very slowly, faith returned to Europe – on the sandaled feet of the white martyrs.

It extended its reach in Europe, moving from there in every direction of the compass, including to the New World, sometimes attended by horrific cruelties. I am sitting on Skellig Michael today, committed to this ancient spiritual quest, only because people like the few monks of this tiny island made the commitments and choices they did. The future of this quest now depends – in part – on the choices of people like me.

There is no guarantee that my faith will survive – either within me or in the world at large. I may find it too difficult or insufficiently satisfying and turn to other things. As may whole continents and cultures.

Europe is again a largely pagan place. Its Christian past is barely a memory to most, and not necessarily a pleasant one at that. The paganism that has replaced it, however, is not like the paganism that preceded it. That ancient paganism always had a spiritual dimension, was always, no matter how clumsily, trying to make contact with spiritual reality.

Present day paganism sometimes tries the same, but more often is blandly secular and consumerist. Unlike both the druids and the Desert Fathers, it embraces the horizontal as the sole reality ("only sky above us" counsels Lennon), replaces the spiritual with the psychological, and is content to deal only with what is in front of our faces. It worships neither gods nor God, but only the shopping mall, the sports palace, the image in the mirror of its self-actualized self. Now there is a desert indeed.

Unfair. A caricature. Self-righteous. I say this to myself even as I write the words above. Okay. But not all together wrong. There is something to this assessment. And I will allow myself these judgments, judgmental though they may seem, as a tip of the hat to my fervent Celtic brethren.

Before its slow retreat into the new paganism, Europe seeded the Americas with faith. And, strangely, as consumerism and nationalism and do-goodism replace the Christian faith in North America, we see Africa and the darker-skinned regions of the world once again becoming fertile soil for passionate pursuit of the things of God. The circle is being completed. What began in the desert is returning to the desert, a place the monks of Skellig Michael would find companionable.

Some tell us—and have been for 200 years—that Christianity is dying—hopelessly outdated, destined to be dug up and puzzled over by distant anthropologists as we do now with Easter Island statues. Others say no, the spiritual is again reasserting itself, as it always will, and it is militant secularism that has had its brief moment in the sun.

Sitting on Skellig Michael, I do not particularly care whether the Vikings or the monks are presently in the ascendancy. I have never placed my bets based on the odds or opinion polls. I feel the pagan instincts of my own life, but also hear the one who stands at the door and knocks. I will make my choices, like the good, individualistic westerner that I am, based on the inclinations of my own heart and the cogitations of my mind—to the extent possible given the vagaries of my will.

✢ ✢ ✢

I did not know what to expect on Skellig Michael, and I am more than pleased at what I've found. After the sea journey and hundreds of steps, I feel I have earned the exhilaration of this view and the satisfaction of imagining monks living and working and worshiping on this bit of holy ground floating in the clouds.

But as usual I am settling for too little. As I consider how long I should sit here with Nate before we head back down, I spot what I should have seen immediately after reaching Christ's Saddle. There, across the way, running up the side of and disappearing behind the north peak, is another set of steps.

I will admit to having mixed feelings about this discovery. I had thought I had arrived. I had done my climb, with the required pilgrimage pain, and had every reason to be satisfied with myself and with what I was experiencing. The views from Christ's Saddle were mind numbing, the imaginative possibilities rich. Why did there need to be more?

Why in fact does there always seem to be more in the spiritual quest? Why does every level of discipline, of service, of intimacy with God seem inadequate? Why do our spiritual guides – living and dead – always call us to go further? Why does our goal always move, mirage-like, just beyond reach?

I find myself too easily satisfied. I am happy enough simply to be on the team. I have no great desire to be a star. Is this humility? Peaceful resting in God's mercy? Perhaps.

More likely spiritual sleepiness. More likely a failure to recognize and follow my own best interests.

I point out the newly-noticed steps to Nate. He is delighted and bounds toward them. We climb up, pass through a short tunnel, and then step onto the place that everyone—except the ignorant and too easily satisfied—comes to Skellig Michael to see.

Here, clinging like an ecclesiastical barnacle to the sheer cliffs, is the tiny monastic village. It comprises six stone huts, two oratories, two cisterns, the foundation of a later medieval church, and a graveyard with eroded stone slabs and crosses. The huts have rectangular bases and beehive-shaped roofs, their flat stones held together only by that accommodation to gravity known as corbelling. Four of them have maintained the structural integrity imparted to them at the time of their making. They still stand fourteen centuries later, without mortar or prop, because they were built realistically. That is, they were built in keeping with the vectors of force inherent in the pull of the earth on everything that aspires to rise above it. They work with, not in defiance of, what is. May your life and mine be so constructed.

On the exterior of the monks' cells, stone pegs protrude here and there. Perhaps they held sod or thatch in place, a small allowance for the harsh winter winds in a place where there were never any fires or hot food or any sources of heat beyond the sun and their own bodies. The lack of warming fire is hard enough to imagine in spring and fall, but think of a harsh, North Atlantic winter. Some speculate that the monks may have left the island in winter, but that is more a testimony to what *we* would do than a reflection of any historical data.

The placement of the monastic site on the southeast side of the north peak, however, may itself have been a minimal concession to comfort. The winds strike the base of the island 600 feet below and ride the stone straight up into the sky. Set back slightly from the cliff face, the cells and oratories enjoy a microclimate that is slightly milder than the rest of the island. It heartens me that perhaps they did not think it a sin to ease the conditions just a bit.

They did not build the monastery here because this site provided a piece of flatness on the island. Only extensive retaining walls, constructed one must imagine with their hearts in their throats, make possible the buildings at this place. Just beyond the outside retaining wall is a long drop into the sea that would give you just enough time to briefly review your relationship with God and man before you entered eternity.

Nate and I look into each cell and then into the larger oratory shaped like an upturned boat. It is dark and does not feel holy. I try to picture the monks here at worship. Their daily offices, the six appointed times of formal worship (a seventh added in the seventh century), centered on recitations from the Psalms, sometimes as many as seventy-five of them in one service. Novices newly entered into the monastic life, usually between the ages of fifteen and seventeen, would have first memorized all of the poems of the Psalter. A mighty feat by our standards – my students think themselves tortured when required to memorize seventy-five words of poetry – but not difficult for an oral culture that preserved all that it knew in the mind and passed it on with the tongue.

In addition to chanting psalms together, the monks would have readings from the Old and New Testament, pray, and sometimes sing hymns. Their prayers were for themselves and the world and the world's leaders. At various times they would perform their worship on their knees with arms outstretched in the crossvigil position, imitating the crucified Christ. Other times they would prostrate themselves completely on the floor.

Nothing about standing in their oratory inclines me to prostrate myself, or even say a prayer. I am not a good pilgrim. The hoped for feelings never come on cue. They did not when once I visited Dachau, another terrible-holy place, and they do not now.

But then I see the little window in the eastern wall. I walk over to it and look out. There in the cemetery just behind the oratory is an ancient cross, apparently marking the grave of one of those early monks. And behind the cross is the sky and sea, and in the sea, like a waiting companion, is Little Skellig.

It strikes me that this view, tiny window framing sea and island (and cross?), has not changed since the day the oratory was enclosed. On that day this space was marked off as a sacred place within a sacred place, a kind of holy of holies. The monks are long-since departed, but perhaps they left behind more than stones.

✤ ✤ ✤

As hard as life must often have been on the monastic

terrace, it was not hard enough for one man. I do not know it at the time, but when I am sitting with Nate on Christ's Saddle at the base of South Peak, I am sitting near to a path that leads up and behind the peak to one of the most precarious hermitages in the world.

Path is not really the right word. It takes rock-climbing skills to reach this place—traverses along narrow ledges with nothing but birds between climber and the sea, handholds and footholds on vertical rock faces. Those with the courage and skill discover a hermitage site composed of three separate small terraces, each seemingly created, as God created the cosmos, *ex nihilo*—out of nothing.

Even looking at photographs of this place gives me a queasy feeling. As one of the few who have studied it closely says, "One views in amazement a fragment of dry-stone wall built by someone who must have been kneeling on the clouds when he placed these stones on a narrow ledge that plummets into what appears to be eternity." Whoever put that first stone on that ledge, just a few dozen feet below the island's peak, also brought—laboriously, bag by bag—shards of rock from other parts of the island to fill in behind the retaining walls and thereby claim a tiny level perch on a sheer rock face that reaches high into the heavens and down into the sea.

Actually, he created three perches. One seems to have been an area for a small garden, a necessity if the hermit was to remain separate from his fellows for long periods. Another, twelve feet above, includes a double water basin carved in stone and the remains of a small oratory—which might also have served as his cell. The reason for the third terrace, the most precarious of all, is a mystery.

I find it significant that from the oratory terrace the hermit could look out across the sky over Christ's Saddle and see on the smaller peak opposite the tops of the beehive huts of his fellow monks. He would have caught glimpses of them at work on the slope above the huts. Did he allow himself to look? Did he long for human contact but reject it as an act of devotion? Or, like his fellow Irishman Jonathan Swift, did his fellow humans disgust him? Was he glad to be free of their contamination? I like to think he sometimes looked over with fondness, maybe even, once or twice, waved.

No one knows who built this hermitage or when, though the best guess is the ninth century, when ascetic extremism flowered in Ireland. Perhaps this hermitage was also a place for the rest of the monks to hide during the Viking raids of that century. But one did not need to build in places the birds would not nest in order to hide from the Vikings. Somebody had a competitive streak.

For some people marathons are not enough, and so they devise one hundred-mile races. Still not enough. So they see who can run the farthest in twenty-four hours. At some point it becomes foolishness (shortly after two miles in my book), but we do not agree where that point is.

The same is true of asceticism in pursuit of the holy. At its best, asceticism is disciplining of the mind and body for the benefit of the soul. At its worst, it is hatred of the created body in a twisted competition whose aim is to manipulate God.

In pagan Ireland, individuals would sometimes fast in order to shame someone – usually someone of superior rank or power—into fulfilling a pledge or giving them justice. Irish political prisoners have retained the weapon to this day. I still recall the news decades ago that the Catholic housewives of Ulster beat the pavement with the lids of garbage cans to spread the word that Bobby Sands had died of hunger in his Northern Ireland prison, on the sixty-sixth day of his political fast.

And it is common in polytheistic religions to perform certain rituals—including fasts—in order to *force* a god to act in a certain way. It's a kind of quid pro quo arrangement. I follow the prescribed forms and the god coughs up the desired action.

After 4,000 years of monotheism, that pagan impulse is still not far away. I will be good and God will bless me. I will be superhumanly devout and God will be forced to bless me supernaturally. I will not just be one of the community, I will be a star, yea, even a saint. If Skellig Michael is a holy place, I will find within it a holier place yet—even if it kills me.

Skellig Michael is dangerous enough without devising further flirtations with death. One nineteenth-century lighthouse operator lost both his sons and a nephew over the cliffs. Another, with a wonderfully terrible verb, referred to the loss of a son who was "clifted" at Seal Cove. Surely some of the monks suffered the same fate.

And one did not have to fall off a cliff to be lost. Sometimes the sea would rise up and snatch you. Consider the wave in December of 1951 that smashed the glass at the lower lighthouse more than 170 feet above the ocean. And then there is the wind.

As a child on the landlocked plains of Texas, I was partial to old hymns about the perils of the sea. On Sunday evenings in small fundamentalist churches I was sure to request, when given the chance, "My Anchor Holds." The words could have been written, though they were not, by Columba or Brendan or a Skellig Michael monk:

> *Though the angry surges roll*
> *On my tempest-driven soul,*
> *I am peaceful, for I know,*
> *Wildly though the winds may blow,*
> *I've an anchor safe and sure,*
> *That can evermore endure.*
> *And it holds, my anchor holds:*
> *Blow your wildest, then, O gale,*
> *On my bark so small and frail;*
> *By His grace I shall not fail,*
> *For my anchor holds, my anchor holds.*

A Texas boy would have known little of angry ocean surges. But perhaps he had some inkling, like the Celtic saints, of what it meant to have a "tempest-driven soul."

Likewise I loved it when my father sang "Ship Ahoy!"– with its thrilling call for rescue from the storm-tossed seas of life. And many times in the 1950s, I watched on television the war documentary *Victory at Sea*. Each time the Navy choir sang the mournful hymn asking the "Eternal Father, strong to save" to rescue "those in peril on the sea," I wanted to cry.

But I could never as a child have pictured an island ship where the waves could reach you at 170 feet. And I could not have further imagined that someone would want to place himself in even more danger at the edge of a cliff almost 700 feet above the water. This testifies to a God-hunger (and hubris?) that is extreme even by Celtic standards.

And yet others followed with a similar craving for spiritual credit. Someone—monk or pilgrim—placed a stone slab at the cloud-kissed tip of South Peak. A narrow ridge at the top has long been called The Spit, but earlier pilgrims called it "the eagle's nest." When Skellig Michael became a popular pilgrimage site after the monks were gone, bonus points were granted for those who risked climbing past the hermitage to edge out on the ridge to kiss the slab. Someone, sometime, scratched on it a small cross. Fortunately perhaps, the slab disappeared in 1977, most likely in an unwitnessed plunge into the sea. We will have to find other ways to get close to God.

Perhaps I am too hard on the South Peak hermit. Perhaps this green martyr was simply a poet of the spirit who needed quiet to hear the rhythms of his soul. I know myself the attraction of solitude. Perhaps our hermit simply felt what another Irish anchorite expressed in a ninth-century poem about his anchorage:

> *In Tuaim Inbhir I find*
> *No great house such as mortals build,*
> *A hermitage that fits my mind*
> *With sun and moon and starlight filled.*

✝ ✝ ✝

As Nate and I sit among the beehive huts, looking over the graves of ancient monks to Little Skellig in the sea

143

beyond, we are joined by fellow pilgrims. Some blond-haired Germans or Scandinavians emerge from the tunnel, perhaps distant relatives of earlier Viking visitors. We nod at each other, separated by language but not, it may be, by quest.

We decide to leave the monastery site to them. Skellig Michael is not a place that improves with company, beyond a friend or two. It's time anyway to return to our boat. I see it down below as we come again to Christ's Saddle and then begin to descend the southern steps.

Part way down, those steps take a sharp turn to the right, and at that point is a protruding weathered rock that I imagine to be a medieval Station of the Cross. I tell Nate to stand in front of it so I can take a picture. He looks a bit Viking-like himself—tall, wild red hair, and cunning smile. I am glad he has come with me on this pilgrimage to Skellig Michael. And I am glad we are leaving.

chapter six

Permanent Pilgrimage – Some Not So Final Thoughts

Do not give your heart to that which does not satisfy your heart.
Abba Poemen

All life is … but a wandering to find home.
Samuel Beckett, *Murphy*

How do you keep a pilgrimage alive? Does it end, or is home simply the next destination?

A visit to Skellig Michael is quite literally a mountaintop experience. Those of us who had figurative mountaintop spiritual experiences as kids in summer church camps know that the trick is to keep alive the mountaintop enthusiasm back in the day-to-day reality of the plains and valleys. In my subculture, it meant going back to school and telling my friends about Jesus. That always seemed like such a good idea when sitting around the campfire, and such an impossible thing once back around the school lunch table. There never seemed a smooth transition from "I'll trade you for that peanut butter and jelly" to "Did you know that Jesus died for your sins?"

What transition, likewise, can there be from Skellig Michael to suburban Saint Paul? I bring home curios and photographs for my friends; what do I bring home for my life? What have I absorbed from this short pilgrimage that will help me on my life-long pilgrimage? Some answers to this question are spread, I think, throughout this book. But certain themes are worth repeating–and worth testing against my daily life.

Much of what I have learned is epitomized in the advice of the desert father: I will give my heart only to those things that satisfy the heart. This, I am finding, requires both a stripping away and a clinging to, and the Celtic Christians are now among my mentors.

One of those mentors is Colman mac Beognae, a student of Columba's, who asked, "What is best for the Christian life?" and answered, "Simplicity and single-mindedness." I hear many people yearning for greater simplicity in their lives, few who have any idea how to achieve it, and fewer still who have tried. Most books on the subject seem to focus on the idea of less, certainly a good idea in a world of excess. But I wonder if we wouldn't do as well to focus on the idea of more–more truth, more wisdom, more reverence, more discipline, more grace.

Simplicity is no great virtue unless wedded to right priorities. A desirable simplicity entails the recognition of what is important in life, coupled with the strength of will to structure one's daily existence around that recognition. It requires minimizing the impact on one's life of unimportant things, an extremely difficult task in an acquisitive and schedule-filling culture.

I don't want to claim too much, but I do believe the Celtic Christians have nudged me a step closer to living simply. I have just finished two weeks of throwing things away in my office. I have won a series of small victories against that inner voice that says, "You sure you want to get rid of that? You never know when you might need it." Flush with these successes, I am now eyeing closets that have stood impregnable for years. I'm even courting heroic thoughts about the garage.

The clutter of things, however, is more easily dealt with than the clutter of the calendar, and the calendar more easily cleared than the mind. I remember the day a colleague appeared in my office doorway many years ago and quoted Kierkegaard to me. "Purity of heart is to will one thing," my colleague said, and then he disappeared. The saints knew this long before Kierkegaard. I am trying to learn it too.

But simplicity is not the default condition of modern life. It does not happen unless it is made. Simplicity is the product of conscious, life-structuring choices. Cuthbert chose to shape his life around prayer and contemplation. Prayer and contemplation were not the norm in medieval Northumbria any more than they are in modern Minnesota. He chose to put them at the center of his daily life because he considered them more important than the alternatives. At times he was pressed to do other things, also important, but he returned to prayer and contemplation whenever possible.

What is there in Cuthbert's example for me? I am too lazy and superficial to make his priorities my own. I comfort myself with the thought that his calling is not my calling—and maybe that is not entirely a rationalization. Instead, I have decided to work less—that is, I hope, to work differently. For nearly twenty years my full-time occupation was teaching. For another ten years I taught part-time and spent the rest working with others on a Bible translation project. That project is now complete, and I have decided to keep a reduced teaching load and spend the rest of the time writing—this book being the first result. It is a kind of simplification, and not without its risks.

For example, Anne, now a teenager, stayed home from school a few weeks back. She watched me write for a stretch at my computer, then move to a chair and read a few pages of a book, then go and sit in the bay window for a while to think while the sun warmed my back. She studied me on the window seat and then asked, "Is this what you do all day?" My wife is more politic, but I suspect she is thinking the same thing.

Can I get away with blaming this on the Celts? They encourage me to simplify my life. They show me that some things are worth taking chances for. They teach me to celebrate the tangible but to value even more the intangible. The intangible, of course, is difficult to eat for dinner, but it can be a banquet for the soul.

✠ ✠ ✠

I am also using my Celtic pilgrimage as an explanation for changing where and how I worship. Delivered and reared by the fundamentalists, shepherded in youth and middle age by the evangelicals, I am now standing, sitting, and kneeling (in what order I'm still not sure) with the liturgicals. Not with the highest of the high church, not with the direct descendents of those who defeated the Celtic ways at the Synod of Whitby, but still with those who recite the ancient prayers, and repeat the creeds, and speak the sacred texts according to the season, and partake each week in holy communion.

In the religious subculture of my childhood, the word *ritual* was almost always preceded by the word *empty*—as in empty rituals. It was what the high churches did—"smells and bells," as a colleague of mine describes it. God, we were sure, was not pleased by this, preferring the hardtack of our own no-nonsense worship. We pretended to serve up fresh batches of reverence each time we came together, but of course we were as wedded to our devotional habits as any richly-robed genuflector. Now, after fifty years on a restricted diet of worship without memory, I feel the need to say words of faith and hope and consolation that believers before me have been saying for centuries.

And the Celts have taught me that worship should spill out of church buildings as water spills out of sacred springs. Worship should be uncontainable, breaking out unbidden in unforeseen encounters with beauty, goodness, or grace. It involves paying attention—understanding the implications of what is happening under my nose and responding appropriately. I am working my way toward seeing all of life as simply different manifestations of worship, and taking these saints as my guide.

They reinforce for me the ancient insight that all things are, or should, be an offering back to the Creator of all things. Gerard Manley Hopkins, from his Celtic location in northern Wales, argued in Celtic style that every created thing had within it a unique signature of its origin in the energy of God. He called that uniqueness "inscape" and counseled us to be on the lookout:

> *The world is charged with the grandeur of God.*
> *It will flame out, like shining from shook foil.*

When one discerns it flaming out, the appropriate response, according to Hopkins and to the Celts long before him, is praise: as in, "Glory be to God for dappled things."

And praise itself is less a conscious act than an ongoing attitude, even a habit of life. The monks—from Skellig Michael to Lindisfarne—memorized the Psalms, came together repeatedly during the day for prayer, and generally organized their lives around God because they wanted to transform worship into instinct. Believing that our fallen nature more spontaneously turns away from rather than toward God, they sought by discipline and repetition to direct their natural impulses back toward the Creator.

And that, they believed, could only be accomplished when the line between worship and daily living was erased. How completely it could be erased, and how at ease they were with their humanness, can be seen in the words of a Celtic monk:

> *I read and write.*
> *I worship my God every day and every night …*
> *I eat little and sleep little.*
> *When I eat, I continue praying,*
> *And when I sleep, my snores are songs of praise.*

If I can learn to make my nightly snores into songs of praise, I will be a holy man indeed.

✠ ✠ ✠

If my pilgrimage has taught me something about simplicity and worship, it has also revealed to me the importance of blessing and being blessed. The Celtic Christians blessed the fire, they blessed the birds, they blessed the night and they blessed the day. But most important, I think, they blessed each other. And so I am trying to do the same.

In direct imitation of these men and women, I have taken to blessing strangers. When I stroll in the mall or sit in the park, I pick people out and say a short prayer of blessing on them. I bless the young and old, the tall and the short, the lean and the fat, the white and the brown. I do the same on freeways and in hallways. I do not do it constantly, because I am often preoccupied. But I do it here and there, and I am trying to make it a habit.

I cannot prove that it does the person I bless—rather, ask blessing for—any good. I cannot explain exactly by what mechanism it *could* do them good, not even in theological terms. But if it does not change them—and I'm not yet willing to give up that hope—it certainly changes me. It makes it less possible for me to have an adversarial relationship to the world. I find myself less annoyed with people and circumstances, less impatient, less desiring that my life be other than it is.

My pilgrimage to sacred places, in short, has increased my sense of gratitude. I am grateful for my life. I am grateful for the dance of nature all about me. I am grateful for kindred spirits (my children among them) and grateful that I am married to a soul-friend. I am grateful for something meaningful to do in life. I am grateful that I still find myself able to accept the existence and the love of a God who created all these other things for which I am grateful.

All of which is to say that if a pilgrim is someone who travels hopefully, who is on a physical journey with a spiritual destination, then I am still a pilgrim, though I have returned home. I am still hopeful, and I am still traveling.

✛ ✛ ✛

Perhaps the oldest metaphor for human existence is life as journey or voyage. A pilgrimage is a richer metaphor yet—if it is a metaphor at all. A pilgrimage is not just movement across space, but a journey with a desirable and attainable destination. It implies companionship, going where others have gone before. It suggests belief in a certain holiness in life—that life is inhabited with meaning and intricacy and spiritual design. It suggests that existence is suffused, ultimately, with presence, that is, with God.

Pilgrimage holds out the possibility that when the last word is spoken about the human experience, it is a benevolent word. Absence, void, and disintegration are real, but not defining. Every good thing is subject to debasement and rupture, but rupture is the offense against the underlying design, not itself the essential nature of things.

Whether this view is hopeful realism or willful delusion is not subject to proof. It is a chosen view of life, one with evidence to support it but without proof to ensure it. It is, with the help of my Celtic guides, the view I choose.

Having declared this my choice, I am obligated to certain actions in life. I believe myself obligated, for instance, to have fewer enemies. Like many, I was struck upon returning from my pilgrimage by the mad, materialistic race that is American society—the unceasing rain of merchandise, malls, and marketing. But I was also more keenly aware of the ceaseless drumbeat of anger and enemy-making.

The right demonizes the left, the left demonizes the right. Progressives are the new Puritans, seeing evil in every nook and cranny of society (not fair to Puritans, I know). Traditionalists see evil only in things that threaten the status quo. And each sees evil most clearly in the other. Leaders are defined now by their ability to frighten and enrage their followers, and nothing does that so well as a vivid and threatening enemy. And all these people want to recruit me to their side, with the ominous warning that if I am not for them, I am against them.

I try, at these times, to think of Aidan. Of the Aidan who gently admonished the colleague who declared the Northumbrians too stubbornly pagan for salvation. Of the Aidan who gave away the king's horse because he wished, like Cuthbert, to "share the conditions" of those to whom he ministered. Of the Aidan who preferred to encourage people to do good rather than to pillory them for doing wrong.

Is it possible to be committed and principled without being factional and predatory? Can I be faithful without being doctrinaire, tolerant without being relativistic? Can I be at the same time a warrior for truth and a river of grace?

Perhaps my new Celtic friends can help. Colman, who

counseled "Simplicity and single-mindedness," also asked, "What is best for the mind?" His answer, again, is helpful:

> *Breadth and humility, for every good thing finds room in a broad, humble mind. What is worst for the mind? Narrowness and closedness and constrictedness, for nothing good finds room in a narrow, closed, restricted mind.*

The modern temperament, of course, approves broad minds, often calling broad (or tolerant) what is, in fact, only absence of standards. But Colman is calling for a kind of temperament that is closer to St. Paul's description of love: patient, kind, not envious or boastful or arrogant or rude, not insisting on its own way or irritable or resentful, not rejoicing in wrong-doing but rejoicing in the truth.

This describes the kind of person I wish to be but am not. I recently engaged in a series of email exchanges with a Hindu activist who wanted to convince me that Christianity would be a much better religion if it was as "flexible" about its claims as Hinduism supposedly is. I pointed out, without rancor but also without much tact, what I thought were the logical inconsistencies in his assertions. As with most of us, this did not please him, and he soon escalated his rhetoric to a vow to defend Hindu culture, by force if necessary, from "arrogant" Christian proselytizers.

Somehow I think Aidan would have done better than I did. I thought it was enough to speak truth, as best I understood it, not realizing sufficiently that truth is merely a sledgehammer in the hands of the unloving. The Celtic Christians changed lives and whole societies without violence or bloodshed. Columba and others seem to have relished head-to-head spiritual battles with their druid counterparts, but they did not believe they should win with the sword what they could not win through the power of the Spirit. The people called them saints because of the kinds of lives they lived, not because they crushed their enemies.

I am searching for balance here–that is, for integrity (wholeness). The Celtic Christians were fiercely committed. They did not carve out stone steps in the cliffs of Skellig Michael because they thought theirs was one of many ways to heaven. They were not flaccid relativists or morally paralyzed like many today who want religion to be nice. But they altered the direction of a significant part of western civilization largely because they lived out their beliefs in the details of their everyday lives, and those around them found that attractive. If activists of all kinds could do the same today, they would have less need for enemies. I will try this myself.

✝ ✝ ✝

What does it mean to say one is always on a pilgrimage? It means, among many things, that one must always be alert. The pilgrim is on the lookout for significance, for signs and rumors of transcendence. I went to Iona expectant, with eyes wide open. I must keep them open now that I have returned.

Ongoing pilgrimage means I must listen to the reports of others who have gone before me and who go with me. It means I must expect obstacles and dead ends and dark nights of the soul. It means I must train my will just as athletes train their bodies: to do instinctively what is in some ways unnatural—or to do what was originally completely natural but no longer seems so.

It means I must look for the holy within the mundane. Ordinariness is the enemy of holiness—unless the ordinary can itself be made holy. If holy means set apart—the *extra*-ordinary—how can that which happens everyday—the ordinary—ever be holy? Only by seeing the holiness hidden within it. Consider the Celtic penchant for washing the smallest routines of daily life with prayer, as in the following words said on covering the coals of the fire each night before going to bed:

> *Lord, preserve the fire, as Christ preserves us all.*
> *Lord, may its warmth remain in our midst, as*
>   *Christ is always among us.*
> *Lord, may it rise to life in the morning, as we shall*
>   *rise with Christ to eternal life.*

Resurrecting the coals in the morning for life-giving fire was no small thing on a winter morning in seventh-century Ireland. But neither, they knew, was being in right relationship with God. And so they linked the two as naturally as birds take flight.

In the journey metaphor, the final end of the journey is death. In pilgrimage the end of the pilgrimage is life—a fuller, richer, truer life than one has previously known. That life, I now suspect, is to be found at what we are inclined to think of as the extremes. It is to be found in paradox. (Less is more. The weak are strong. Foolishness is wisdom. The first shall be last. Those who lose their lives shall find them.) It is to be found in mystery, and contrariness, and trust.

The clues for such a life abide in small piles of stone on little islands in out-of-the way places only pilgrims bother to seek. Let those with eyes to see, see.

✝ ✝ ✝

Will I ever be as close to God as it seems were the men and women of Iona, Lindisfarne, Durham, Ely, Norwich, St. David's, Kildare, Glendalough, Skellig Michael, and countless other places I know nothing about? Do I want to be? Am I as much a tourist in faith as I am a tourist in these places? Am I not one of Eliot's sleepers under the snow feeding just a little life with dried tubers? Am I not eager to believe that these people were reclusive extremists, altogether too ascetic, altogether too unbalanced in pursuit of a God who may not in fact be there anyway?

And were they truly any closer to God after all? We know, or think we know, that the stories about them are too good and too miraculous to be true. We know that they themselves weren't impressed with their own holiness. And given that good and great people have always been found to have feet of clay, it is not reasonable to assume that living on a mountain peak or sleeping with a stone pillow, or praying in frigid water, or fasting like Kafka's hunger artist is enough, or even helpful, to purify the spirit.

And yet there is something we also know about them. We know that they inclined their lives toward God in the hope and expectation that God had already inclined toward them. Today we have built huge radio telescopes on mountaintops on the off chance that someone or something somewhere out in the galactic dust is trying to say something to us. The odds are extremely long but representatives of the human race sit every day waiting for a message.

Columba, and those like him, were doing the same thing on better grounds. They organized their thoughts and their habits to become instruments for the reception of spiritual information. God has sent messages to Mount Sinai and to Bethlehem and to many other places in the world. Why not to Iona? Why not to Skellig Michael? And if to Skellig Michael, why not to Minnesota, where I find myself most of the time? But is Minnesota listening? Do we have our antennae out? Am I inclining my life in God's direction?

I didn't need to go to Iona to find the holy, and in fact I didn't find it, because I didn't bring it with me. What I did find was more about the possibilities of living attentively, about how one might structure a life – and I don't mean the monastic rule itself–to increase the potential for giving that life meaning and purpose. I learned something about stripping away superficialities, about discipline, about desire and freedom from desire, about singleness of purpose – about God hunger.

Eliot ends "Little Gidding" with a series of paradoxes, each with the ring of the biblical paradox that those who would find their lives must lose them. One of them, often quoted, speaks of continuous exploration that will find it has returned to where it started "and know the place for the first time."

My physical pilgrimage to these holy places is over for now, but my pilgrimage through life goes on. I think I know why these people were wanderers–in body and in spirit–and I think I know why we travel to see where they went. Like us, they were looking for the city that has no foundations, and we are hoping they have left us clues. We are all pilgrims because we all have a yearning for home– and the feeling that we're not quite there yet. But because I've been to Iona and Lindisfarne and Skellig Michael, and places like them, I feel more prepared to recognize the place when I see it.

SELECTED BIBLIOGRAPHY

These are some of the books I read while traveling or shortly after my return. There is no pretense that these represent the most important books on the topic. They are simply the ones I came across. Most factual assertions come from one or more of these books.

GENERAL

Bitel, Lisa M. *Isle of the Saints: Monastic Settlement and Christian Community in Early Ireland*. Ithaca: Cornell UP, 1990.

Bradley, Ian. *Celtic Christianity: Making Myths and Chasing Dreams*. Edinburgh: Edinburgh UP, 1999.

Cremin, Aedeen. *The Celts*. New York: Rizzoli, 1998.

Davies, Oliver, and Thomas O'Loughlin. *Celtic Spirituality*. New York: Paulist Press, 1999.

Finaldi, Gabriele. *The Image of Christ*. London: National Gallery, 2000.

Catalogue of exhibition *Seeing Salvation* at the National Gallery (London), 26 February–7 May 2000.

Matthews, Caitlin. *The Little Book of Celtic Blessings*. Shaftesbury: Element, 1994.

Myers, Robert Manson. *Handel's Messiah: A Touchstone of Taste*. New York: Macmillan, 1948.

Ola, Per and Emily D'Aulaire. "Inscribing the Word." *Smithsonian* 31 (December 2000): 78-88.

Robinson, Martin. *Rediscovering the Celts: The True Witness from Western Shores.* London: Fount, 2000.

———.*Sacred Places, Pilgrim Paths: An Anthology of Pilgrimage.* London: Fount, 1998.

Rodgers, Michael and Marcus Losack. *Glendalough: A Celtic Pilgrimage.* Black Rock, Ireland: Columba Press, 1996.

Sellner, Edward C. *Wisdom of the Celtic Saints.* Notre Dame, Indiana: Ave Maria Press, 1993.

Young, Percy M. *Messiah: A Study in Interpretation.* London: Dennis Dobson, 1951.

IONA

Adomnan of Iona, *Life of St Columba.* Trans. by Richard Sharpe. London: Penguin, 1995.

MacArthur, E. Mairi. *Columba's Island: Iona from Past to Present.* Edinburgh: Edinburgh UP, 1995.

Mackworth-Praed, Ben. *The Book of Kells.* London: Studio, 1993.

Millar, Peter W. *Iona.* Norwich: Canterbury Press, 1997.

Meehan, Bernard. *The Book of Kells: An Illustrated Introduction to the Manuscript in Trinity College Dublin.* London: Thames and Hudson, 1994.

Ritchie, Anna. *Iona.* London: Batsford, 1997.

Roy, James Charles. *Islands of Storm.* Chester Springs, Pa.: Dufour, 1991.

Watteville, Alastair de. *The Isle of Iona: Sacred, Spectacular, Living.* Hampshire: Romsey Fine Art, 1999.

Watts, Murray. *The Wisdom of Saint Columba of Iona*. Oxford: Lion, 1997.

LINDISFARNE

Backhouse, Janet. *The Lindisfarne Gospels: A Masterpiece of Book Painting.* London: The British Library, n.d.

O'Sullivan, Deirdre, and Robert Young. *Lindisfarne: Holy Island.* London: Batsford, 1995.

Van de Weyer, Robert, ed. *Bede: Celtic and Roman Christianity in Britain.* Berkhampsted: Arthur James, 1997.

SKELLIG MICHAEL

Horn, Walter, and Jenny White Marshall, Grellan D. Rourke. *The Forgotten Hermitage of Skellig Michael.* Berkeley: U California P, 1990.

Lavelle, Des. *The Skellig Story: Ancient Monastic Outpost.* Dublin: O'Brien Press, 1993.

———. *The Skellig Experience.* n.p.: Cork Kerry Tourism, n.d.

Moorhouse, Geoffrey. *Sun Dancing: A Vision of Medieval Ireland.* New York: Harcourt Brace, 1997.

ONLINE RESOURCES

Rather than directing the reader to numerous specific websites, which have a habit of disappearing into the ether, I suggest doing a name or image search using a good search engine, such as Google. Type in names from the book—such as Iona, Lindisfarne, Skellig Michael, Columba, *Book of Kells,* and so on—and enjoy the many stunning photographs and engaging discussions of all these things.

FURTHER SUGGESTIONS

Stanley Spencer's "Christ Carrying the Cross" can be found through the Tate Gallery website: www.tate.org.uk

A CD-ROM of the *Book of Kells* can be ordered from Trinity Library, Dublin: www.tcd.ie/Library/Visitors/kells.htm

A detail of the cats and mice (or are they kittens?) on the Chi-Rho page of the *Book of Kells* can be found as follows: www.nd.edu/~medvllib/facsintro/irishmss/details/d3.html

Information about and images of the Lindisfarne Gospels can be found at the British Library website: www.bl.uk/collections/treasures/lindis.html.

PHOTOGRAPHY NOTES

Location of and credit for photographs are as follows.

COVER: Steps from Christ's Saddle to the monastic terrace on Skellig Michael. Daniel Perego

INSIDE FLAP: The author at Little Skellig. Nate Taylor

TITLE PAGE: The author in St. Mary the Virgin parish church on Lindisfarne. Matthew Taylor

PAGE 8: South Peak of Skellig Michael, near the top of which were the hermitage and the cross-etched slab. Daniel Taylor

PAGE 14: Looking east from Dun I on Iona across the sound to the island of Mull. Barbara Leafblad

PAGE 40: Cross near Iona Cathedral, looking toward the sound. Barbara Leafblad

PAGE 66: Wooden poles at Lindisfarne marking the walking path across the mud flats that pilgrims follow at low tide. ©FreeFoto.com

PAGE 86: Tower in the monastic city at Glendalough. Barbara Leafblad

PAGE 114: Looking out of oratory window on Skellig Michael toward Little Skellig. Daniel Taylor

PAGE 146: Sculpture of monks in a boat on Ring of Kerry. Daniel Taylor

PAGE 162: Stone buildings on cliff's edge on the monastic terrace on Skellig Michael. Des Lavelle

PAGE 166: Celtic cross at Cashel. Barbara Leafblad

PAGE 168: Statue of Aidan at church of St. Mary the Virgin on Lindisfarne. Barbara Leafblad

Also by DANIEL TAYLOR